monetary freedom, when it truly earned the title "land of opportunity."

Only in 1933, when the United States unwisely went off the gold standard, Ms. Snyder says, did our present seemingly unending series of economic troubles begin, follow... ...relations ... of an ever... croaches e... rights of th...

With fine... new light to... ...ood subject. Her und... ...ding of capitalism and economics offers superb insight. *Why Gold?* is an immensely readable book that not only shows where America has gone wrong but offers a workable plan for economic stability and a successful return to the gold standard.

ABOUT THE AUTHOR

Leslie Snyder, born in New Jersey and reared in California, graduated from high school as a mathematics major. After one year of college accounting, she went to work as a bookkeeper. Six years later, she was a top-paid, full-charge bookkeeper, had her own income tax practice and was self-employed. Seeking new challenge, she started studying philosophy and psychology to find out more about herself. Because of her math and business background, she says, she fell in love with economics, which led her to gold. With her husband she built a successful investment business. She now lives in Oxnard, California, where her hobbies, appropriately enough, include coin collecting.

Why Gold?

DATE DUE

DE 03 '96			
NO 21 '96			

WHY GOLD?

**The One Sure Cure for Inflation
and Economic Tyranny**

By

LESLIE SNYDER

An Exposition-University Book

EXPOSITION PRESS   NEW YORK

To George Conway

First Edition

© 1974 by Leslie Snyder

Library of Congress Catalog Card Number: 73-92853

ISBN 0-682-47884-9

Manufactured in the United States of America

CONTENTS

INTRODUCTION

This speech has been attributed to John Adams, the second President of the United States of America, in his fight for American independence.

Sink or swim, live or die, survive or perish, I give my hand and my heart to this vote . . . Sir, I know the uncertainty of human affairs, but I see, I see clearly, through this day's business. You and I, indeed, may rue it. We may not live to see the time when this Declaration shall be made good . . . But whatever may be our fate, be assured, be assured, that this Declaration will stand . . .

Sir, before God, I believe the hour is come. My judgment approves this measure, and my whole heart is in it. All that I have, and all that I am, and all that I hope in this life, I am now ready here to stake upon it; and I leave off as I began, that live or die, survive or perish, I am for the Declaration. It is my living sentiment, and by the blessing of God it shall be my dying sentiment: independence now, and INDEPENDENCE FOREVER.

Independence! That is why we fought the American Revolution; that is why fifty-six men pledged their lives and their fortunes. Blood was shed, lives lost, and property destroyed. All this for the cause of freedom and independence. Independence! This is the essence of being an American.

No group of men ever understood the importance of independence more than our Founding Fathers. So well they knew the history of the rise and fall of great nations, that they founded the new country squarely and firmly on the Gold Standard.

The Gold Standard embodies the principles of monetary freedom and independence. The issue of hard money (the gold standard) versus paper money was the most important issue of the post-Revolutionary era. In fact, the Gold Standard issue has raged from the time of the Revolution to the present.

The four words "not worth a Continental" recall the paper money that caused the runaway inflation that very nearly destroyed the American Revolution. And as a result of that turbulent and devastating era, the framers of the Constitution made only gold and silver lawful tender in payment of debts.

During the Civil War, seventy-five years later, Congress enacted a legal tender law, which again forced Americans to accept paper money, and the country entered another inflationary era. Thirteen years later, in 1875, by an act of Congress, hard money payments were resumed.

Fifty-eight years later by Executive Order of April 5, 1933, Franklin D. Roosevelt prohibited hard money—gold coins, gold bullion, and gold certificates from the recognized and customary channels of trade and required same to be delivered to member banks of the Federal Reserve System.

This amounted to government confiscation of private property. Never before in American history had Americans been prohibited from owning gold. During the Revolution hard money became scarce because of the abundance of paper money. During the Civil War the Western states, especially California, used hard money for trade. But gold was always freely owned.

The reason why the Gold Standard issue has raged for the greater part of two centuries is simply that the majority of Americans do not understand it. But the importance of the Gold Standard cannot be overemphasized. It is crucial for the maintenance and improvement of our high standard of living.

During the 146 years of monetary freedom, from 1787 to 1933, America grew and prospered. Capitalism spread from country to country. The standard of living throughout the industrialized world rose to unprecedented heights. But more important was the fact that the price level of all goods and services during this same time period remained stable. The reasons for this remarkable rate of stable growth were clear: the capitalistic productive system and the stable dollar, which was "as good as gold."

Since 1933, however, Americans have been prohibited from

owning gold. This ill-advised action is producing today its pre-dictable results—runaway inflation, oppressive taxation, chronic unemployment, the growth of big government, disrespect for life and property, lack of patriotism, and moral disintegration.

It seems that ignorance about the nature of money has existed in America since the Revolution. In 1829, John Quincy Adams, son of John Adams and sixth President of the United States, observed that "all the perplexities, confusion and distress in America arise, not from defects in their constitution or confederation, not from want of honor or virtue, so much as from down-right ignorance of the nature of coin, credit, and circulation."

History, it seems, has not only proved John Quincy Adams correct, but it appears as though history is repeating itself.

In the two hundred years since American independence, the United States has made the round trip, from inflation and oppressive taxation to monetary freedom, and today we are back to inflation and oppressive taxation. (Must we fight another revolution before we win back our birthright—monetary freedom?)

There must be a renaissance in monetary thinking if the United States is to break out of the monetary whirlpool in which it is sinking. If we want to maintain our high standard of living for which we have worked so long and so hard, we must return to the stability and justice of the Gold Standard.

This course of thinking is contrary to the popular trend of our times. But when the Gold Standard was supreme and unde-featable, monetary sanity reigned.

The purpose of this book, therefore, is to dispel the ignorance surrounding the nature of coin, credit, and circulation. It shows how to stop inflation and its destructive results, and how to return to monetary freedom and sanity—the Gold Standard.

Oxnard, California   Leslie Snyder
September 17, 1973

PART I

MAN'S RIGHTS AND GOLD

1

THE DECLARATION OF INDEPENDENCE

In 1776, fifty-six men joined together to declare the independence of man. This was the first time in history that man had declared that he possessed certain "unalienable rights." Those fifty-six men declared: "We hold these truths to be self-evident; that all men are created equal; that they are endowed by their creator with certain unalienable rights; that among these are life, liberty, and the pursuit of happiness . . ." The self-evident truths which the fifty-six men, the Founding Fathers, proclaimed were man's right to live by reason, to choose the purpose of his happiness, and to keep the fruits of his labor. The crucial principle that the Founding Fathers discovered was that man's happiness lay with man, the individual—that man is an end in himself—not the means to the ends of others. These men produced the greatest document the world had ever seen. They produced the American Declaration of Independence.

Thomas Jefferson, author of the Declaration, said the purpose of the Declaration is "to place before mankind the common sense of the subject" and to make this document "an expression of the American mind."

The Declaration, as "an expression of the American mind," concisely states man's rights and defines the purpose and nature of government. It declares:

> . . . that to secure these rights, governments are instituted among men, deriving their just powers from the consent of the governed; that whenever any form of government becomes destructive to these ends, it is the right of the people to alter or to abolish it, and to institute new government, laying its foundation on such principles, and organizing its powers in such form, as to them shall seem most likely to effect their

safety and happiness . . . when a long train of abuses and usurpations pursuing invariably the same object, evinces a design to reduce them under absolute despotism, it is their right, it is their duty, to throw off such government and to provide new guards for their future security.

The Declaration also declares that ". . . all experience hath shown that mankind are more disposed to suffer while evils are sufferable, than to right themselves by abolishing the forms to which they are accustomed." Jefferson's observation was correct. It took 6,000 years of agonizing history before the people cried: "Enough! Enough of the divine right of kings; enough of inquisitions, the tyranny of the mob; enough of bureaucratic whim and of super planners!"

The American colonists rebelled at the idea of being the means by which King George III ruled their lives. They rebelled at the idea of "taxation without representation," that they should be taxed to support British troops they never requested nor wanted, which were to be garrisoned in the colonies. They rebelled at British interference in their trade with the Navigation Acts, the Stamp Act, the Townshend Acts, and the Intolerable Acts.

In every stage of these oppressions the colonists petitioned for redress. But their petitions were answered only by repeated injury.

Emotions were running high. It would not have taken much to bring a showdown between the colonists and the garrisoned British troops. The colonists were already fired up by Patrick Henry's "Give Me Liberty or Give Me Death" speech. And when Paul Revere warned them of oncoming British troops, the colonists readied themselves. They foiled the attempted arrest of Samuel Adams and John Hancock. Interference in the colonists' lives culminated in 1776 at Lexington and Concord, when the first shots of the American Revolution were fired.

By 1776, the fifty-six Founding Fathers realized that there was to be no liberty and justice under British rule. They were ready to take a stand—to dissolve all political connection between them and the State of Great Britain. On July 4, 1776, standing tall, straight, and unwavering, they solemnly published and declared, "that these United Colonies are, and of right ought to be, free and independent States; that they are absolved from all allegiance to the British Crown . . . And for the support of this declaration . . . we mutually pledge to each other our lives, our fortunes, and our sacred honor."

The price for freedom and independence came high. It cost some of the Founding Fathers their lives and their fortunes. Here was the result: Five signers were captured by the British as traitors. Twelve had their homes ransacked and burned. Two lost their sons in the Continental Army. Another had two sons captured. Nine of the fifty-six signers fought and died from wounds or the hardships of the American Revolution. But the honor of all fifty-six men survived unscathed, to be remembered with a feeling of pride by all future Americans.

These are the stories typical of those who risked everything to sign the Declaration of Independence. They were not wild-eyed, rabble-rousing ruffians. They were heroes, men larger than life, who distinguished themselves by bravery. Twenty-five men were lawyers or jurists. Eleven were merchants. Nine were farmers or large plantation owners. They were men of means and education. They had security, but they valued liberty more. They signed the Declaration of Independence knowing full well that the penalty could be death if they were captured.[1]

"There is a price tag on human liberty," said James Monroe. "That price is being free men. Payment of this price is a personal matter with each of us." Benjamin Franklin summed it up when he said, "They that can give up essential liberty to obtain a little temporary safety, deserve neither liberty nor safety." No, freedom is not free. The price is very high indeed.

To secure the rights for which the revolutionists fought and died, the Founding Fathers produced another great document— The Constitution of the United States of America. William Pitt said, "It will be the wonder and admiration of all future genera-

---

[1] "The Price They Paid," a speech given at Independence Hall, Knott's Berry Farm, Buena Park, California, 1972.

tions and the model of all future constitutions." The English statesman William Gladstone described it as "the most perfect work ever struck off at a given point in time, by the brain and purpose of man."

The Founding Fathers took much care to make sure that the essence of the Constitution was clear, that government should have limited power, because the Founding Fathers had a deep suspicion of all governments. They believed that one of the great threats to a man's life, liberty and property had always been the government under which he lived. They believed that all governments would, if permitted, enslave the people, always with the excuse of "taking care" of the people. In the words of George Washington, "Government is not reason, it is not eloquence; it is force. Like fire, which if it is not controlled, will destroy you." Thomas Jefferson said, "That Government is best which governs least."

Based on their deep suspicion of governments, the Founding Fathers intentionally subordinated government to the individual. The individual can do anything he wishes, except that which infringes upon another individual's rights; government can do only that which the Constitution allows it to do.

The Founding Fathers knew that government's actions must be limited because it holds a monopoly over force. Since only by force can man's rights be abrogated, they purposely wrote the Constitution so that it protects man's rights. *The protection of man's rights from force is the only moral function of government.* Thus, the purpose of the armed forces is to protect man from foreign invasion, the police force from criminals, and the court system from fraud—to protect and enforce contracts which are a prerequisite in a higher form of civilization.

Constitutionalism is the only moral government because it is based on and limited by individual rights. Individual rights start with the right to one's life—the basic and essential right, which makes all other rights possible. The right to one's property and the right to keep the fruits of one's labor implement the right to one's life because they are the means by which one sustains his life and pursues his happiness.

The alternative to property rights, or no property rights, is slavery. It is either-or. This is the right to take action, not the right to an object. There is no guarantee that a man will earn any property, only the guarantee that he will own it if he earns it. There can be no right to the right of the fruits of the labor of others, because this means that those others are deprived of rights and condemned to slave labor. There can be no such thing as the right to enslave or the right to destroy rights.

So that man will know what his rights are the Constitution provides him with objective, well-defined laws.

The opposite of limited constitutional government is unlimited government, or socialism, statism, communism, Fascism, Marxism, and totalitarianism. Under socialism man has no rights—government is supreme. It has the right to subject the people to absolute rule. What man creates, government disposes. Thus, no property rights.

The third type of government, or no government, is anarchy, where no moral standards or objective laws exist.

Constitutional government is designed to protect man's inalienable rights from government force, coercion, and interference. This is the meaning of the principle of political freedom. It is the only valid justification of a government. The Bill of Rights was designed to declare explicitly that individual rights supersede any public or social power, by further limiting the power of government. It reinforced man's supremacy over government and society. It was designed by the American people, who had been trained for generations to be jealous of their freedoms.

At the close of the Constitutional Convention, Benjamin Franklin was asked, "What is the kind and form of our government?" He answered, "A Republic—if you can keep it!"

The Founding Fathers never faltered in their conviction that it was a republic they cherished, not a democracy. As Alexander Hamilton said, "We are a Republican Government. Real liberty is never found in a despotism or in the extremes of Democracy." The dangers of democracy were also well understood by James Madison, who said, "Democracies have ever been found incompatible with personal security, or the rights of property; and have in general been as short in their lives as they have been violent in their deaths."

The supreme spokesman for liberty in American colonial life, Thomas Jefferson, looked ahead to future generations and wondered: "Yes, we did produce a near perfect Republic, but will they keep it, or will they in the enjoyment of plenty, lose the memory of freedom? Material abundance without character is the surest way to destruction."

Thomas Jefferson certainly knew what he was talking about. Destruction of life and property is rampant today. And the reason can be traced to the lack of character, or the philosophy, of the majority of Americans.

Although our inalienable rights were declared in 1776 and established in 1787, their philosophic and economic principles have yet to be understood by the large majority of Americans. Ignorance is not bliss; it is dangerous. Since America deviated from the principles of the Constitution, especially in economics, inflation, taxation and destruction are symptomatic of today's problems.

The Founding Fathers had suffered from oppressive taxation and inflation and fought to free themselves from their unjust and injurious consequences. They understood how tryanny begins with encroachment on private property. So they conceived of a nation where men were free to keep what they earned, where no oppressive taxation robbed them of their earnings, where no inflation embezzled their hard-earned savings. Their idea of freedom meant absolute and total freedom, not only from political tyranny, but also from economic tyranny.

These men were heroes. They fought the American Revolution to free themselves from political and economic tyranny. They sacrificed the present for the future, a feat few men can claim. To secure their property from future government encroachment, they produced the Declaration of Independence and the Constitution. To further secure their property as best they could, they made *only* gold and silver lawful money.

In fact, gold and silver money was as important to the

Founding Fathers as were their other rights. Gold and silver money was incorporated into the body of the Constitution before the Bill of Rights was written. Only gold and silver money was acceptable to them because it secured their economic freedom, which, in turn, secured their political freedom. Political freedom requires economic freedom. And economic freedom requires monetary freedom.

The next two chapters explain the truths that were implicit in the Declaration's self-evident truths that man has a right to life, liberty, and pursuit of happiness.

The remaining chapters explain what should have been explicit in the Constitution, that to secure the inalienable rights to which Americans have a right (and to rid the country of the lethal consequences of inflation), there are two requirements of society. The first requirement is a proper economic system, which is Capitalism. The second requirement is a proper monetary system, which is gold.

2

THE FOUNDING FATHERS' PHILOSOPHY

The self-evident truths to which the Declaration and the Constitution refer are based on a philosophy whose highest value is life—man's life.

Man, unlike the animal, has the choice of whether or not to live. An animal naturally hunts for his food—his only basic need. Man's basic needs—food, clothing, and shelter—must first be produced before consumed. Their production is a lifetime endeavor. To produce them, man must think. And to think efficiently, man must have a philosophy.

The philosophy of the Founding Fathers is the philosophy of individual rights. It can enable man to know how to produce his basic needs efficiently, how to keep the fruits of his labor, what his rights are, and how to protect them. This philosophy can insure man's rights to life, liberty, and the pursuit of happiness.

The Founding Fathers were well educated in philosophy. They were mostly second-generation Americans, schooled in individual rights and profoundly dedicated to the preservation of the rights of free men. They were raised with a deep respect for science and the "natural law." Their basic philosophical principles of life were founded by the seventeenth-century philosopher John Locke.

Those principles were based on a philosophy which strived to understand reality and the laws of nature. Some of the key ideas of political thought at the time of the Constitutional Convention were: Man's rights flow from nature—natural, inalienable and essential to meaningful existence. The greatest rights were life (self-preservation), liberty, property (to use and dispose of the fruits of one's labor), and happiness. A good society existed where natural rights were recognized and protected and that was the purpose of government. The best form of government was

11

republican—representative and responsible. Possibly the most important idea was that the people always retain the right of resistance as a last refuge.[1]

In addition to a strong respect for reality and the search for truth, they respected man's mind, the reasoning faculty that enables him to grasp reality. Reason is man's basic tool of survival.

Thomas Jefferson understood the tremendous reasoning power of the mind. He believed that the meaning of the "pursuit of happiness" was toward the achievement of a balanced life— the harmony of mind, body and spirit, of thought and action, with a resulting serenity and sense of well-being. His adherence to reason over force was exhibited through his admiration of the Constitution, which he conveyed in a letter to David Humphreys on March 18, 1789:

> The example of changing a constitution by assembling the wise men of the state, instead of assembling armies, will be worth as much to the world as the former examples we had given them. The constitution, too, which was the result of our deliberation, is unquestionably the wisest ever yet presented to men.

Men such as Thomas Jefferson, George Washington, James Madison, John Adams, and Benjamin Franklin, were men of principles. They were statesmen; they considered the future first, the present second. It was their confidence in man's mind, his rationality, that forms the basis of the Constitution and of the concept of man's inalienable right to life. Because the Founding Fathers believed man was good—a value unto himself—they demanded his freedom, so that he could earn his living as he saw fit.

They believed that man possessed "free will." He was able to think, to know right from wrong, and thus he was able to deal

---

[1]Clinton Rossiter, *1787 The Grand Convention* (New York: The Macmillan Co., 1966), pp. 61-63.

successfully with reality. When they proclaimed that man, the individual, superseded government, they threw off the control of men over men; they discovered political and economic freedom! As an unprecedented phenomenon in history, the Founding Fathers were thinkers and men of action! It was because of their benevolent philosophy and their will to do right based on inalienable, natural rights—unchanging principles—two hundred years ago, that Americans today enjoy their constitutional freedoms.

Since the concept of rights is vital to man's survival, the definition of the word "rights" should be clearly understood. A "right" is a moral principle that defines and sanctions a man's freedom of action in society. The one fundamental right that makes all other rights possible is the right to one's life. This is the right to take the action that will sustain and further one's life. This is essential to man as a condition to life as his nature demands. This is freedom of action—to be free from force and coercion by other men or government. Therefore, a right sanctions a positive action—freedom to think, judge, and act for every individual by his own voluntary, uncoerced choice.

The concept of individual rights is so prodigious a feat of political thinking that few men grasp it fully—and two hundred years have not been enough for other countries to understand it. But this is the concept to which men owe their lives—the concept which made it possible for them to bring into existence everything of value that anyone ever did or ever will produce, achieve, or experience.

The concept of individual rights manifests itself in the right to property, the only means by which to implement the right to life. Property rights allow man to take the action that is required to sustain his life. Knowing he can keep what he earns, man can plan long-range. This is important to man because he is unable to live like an animal, on the range of the immediate moment. Some projection of the future is a necessity of man's survival. Rights to life and property are inalienable rights. To alienate man from his rights is to alienate him from his life.

Political freedom and economic freedom mean the right to life and property. Political freedom requires economic freedom—

separate state and economics. The only moral economic system is capitalism—the private ownership of the means of production. Laissez-faire capitalism, which is true economic freedom, means a totally unregulated and uncontrolled economy, free exchange of goods and services. Laissez-faire capitalism means freedom to think and the right to property—the translation of one's thoughts into action.

When one grasps the principles of the American philosophy of individual rights, one can understand the concepts that are required of a free society. One can understand the importance of free trade, the right to the fruits of one's labor and the destructive results of government interference in both. One can grasp why political and economic freedom require the right to property —especially the individual right to own and trade gold.

Ask any socialist about gold—he knows why it must be destroyed as a standard of value in order to further the socialist cause. But Americans do not know why it is patriotic to own gold. They do not know why only the private ownership of gold, an inalienable right, can guard their life, liberty, and pursuit of happiness. The Founding Fathers' philosophy explains the importance of gold. The right to own gold is the difference between freedom and slavery.

3

MAN WORKS FOR PROFIT AND PLEASURE

Man's basic needs must be produced before they can be consumed, of course. Production is the application of reason to the problem of survival. Life is a process of self-sustaining and self-generated action. When man works he is converting his energy—both mental and physical—into products or services that will sustain and enhance his life.

Although man must produce, productive work is one of man's most fundamental areas of pleasure. This is because through his work, man gains his basic sense of control over his life. And in controlling his life, he earns his self-confidence—confidence in his mind. The feeling of confidence that comes from knowing that one is able to think, to achieve and to meet and overcome new challenges is pleasurable.

To experience pleasure is very important to man. It is a profound psychological need. Through the state of enjoyment, man experiences the value of life, the sense that life is worth living, worth struggling to maintain. Pleasure serves as the emotional fuel to propel him onward to greater achievements.

Just as pleasure is the reward of successful action, pain, on the other hand, is a signal of danger. Pain is the penalty of unsuccessful action and implies the feeling of helplessness. The continuation of pain and suffering will lead to failure, destruction and death.

Therefore, since the activity of pursuing and achieving values or goals is the essence of the life-process, happiness or suffering may be regarded as an "incentive system" built into man, a system of reward and punishment, designed to further and protect man's life.[1]

---

[1]Nathaniel Branden, *The Psychology of Self-Esteem* (Los Angeles: Nash Publishing Corp., 1969), p. 70.

Since man must work and his work can be of immense pleasure, it stands to reason that he should choose the career which he thinks will be the most rewarding.

The first choice that man must make is between working on a self-sustaining farm or joining the division of labor in society. On the farm his production is limited. But by gaining two benefits from society—knowledge and trade—he can expand his knowledge, learn more, produce more and thereby raise his standard of living. If he devotes his effort to a special field, while others do the same, there is a greater return on production. The division of labor in society raises everybody's standard of living.

Assuming man is free to choose the career from which he thinks he will derive the utmost happiness, and he chooses to live and work in society, certain conditions of society are required in order for him to function efficaciously in the division of labor. The first condition is that man must be allowed to live by reason. That is, he must be free to think, to produce, and to trade without force or coercion. When no force is permitted, discussion, persuasion, and voluntary agreement or disagreement prevail. He must be free to trade with whom he chooses, when he chooses, and for how much he chooses. The market must be free to determine the price of all products and wages. Society must be completely free from government interference—separate state and economics.

Where society is free from government interference, (freedom implies free from government coercion), man can earn from his work his two most important rewards. For man will only work if he has something to gain from it. (Slave labor is not the American way.) The first reward is material. The harder a man works the more he produces. This brings more wealth into existence. As man's efficiency increases his profit increases, and the wealthier he becomes. This is the American way.

The other reward man earns from his work is intangible. It is the emotional pleasure that comes from doing a good job, from being productive and being able to survive. Competence in his work earns man his self-respect. And, together, self-confidence and self-respect earn man his self-esteem, which is a basic psychological need for survival.

A free society attracts men of ambition and productiveness. A free society is a prerequisite to a high standard of living. Only where man is free to choose his life's work, able to advance in his work as far as his ability can take him, and able to retain the material rewards of his labor, can he experience the pleasure that he has rightfully earned.

Profit and pleasure are the incentives that drive man onward to greater achievements. There is no better way to retain profit—earnings, savings, and investments—than by receiving payment in gold. Gold is practically indestructible; it cannot rust, corrode or tarnish. The fleeting energy of man can thus be preserved and transformed into enduring gold.

4

WHAT IS MONEY?

All self-supporting men work to convert their mental and physical energy into products or services so that they may obtain value for their effort. Since man must produce to survive and money is what he is paid for his labor, it is important to know what money is, and, in particular, what good money is.

In olden days, to a cobbler, plying his craft from a bench under a tree, money was a gold coin, of relatively pure content. Saved at the end of a day, it was a financial reserve, and his bank was his wife's arms and ankles, which he could encircle with these savings. The bracelets and anklets of coins afforded security against famine, depression, or old age, and they might provide the capital whereby he could graduate from the ranks of a street cobbler and acquire his own shop, and from there progress to affluence, as far as his ambition would take him. But when he could no longer save a piece of gold, but had to accept instead a piece of paper that if saved could be eaten by termites or destroyed by rain, and in any case, depreciated from month to month, then his hopes for rising in the world were cut off and he became a prey to unrest and revolutionary plotting.

In essence, money is the means of survival. And good, hard money is the means to freedom, independence, and wealth. Soft, depreciating money leads to poverty, slavery, unrest, and revolution.

Philosophically, money is the material shape of the principle that men who wish to deal with one another must deal by trade and give value for value. Since man's mind is the root of all the goods produced and of all the wealth that has ever existed on earth, money is tribute to the glory of man.

Money is the means of survival for free men. To condemn money is to condemn one's life. To abandon money is to embrace force and coercion. The man who respects money has earned it.

There is only one society, one country, that is a "country of money"—the United States of America. Americans have the distinction that no other nation can claim, the fact that they are the people who created the phrase "to make money." Previously, men had always thought of wealth as a static quantity—to be seized, begged, inherited, shared, looted or obtained as a favor. Americans are the first to understand that wealth has to be created. Money is made—before it can be expropriated and redistributed—made by the effort of every honest man, each to the extent of his ability.

When money ceases to be the tool by which men deal with one another, only one arbiter remains—the gun. A society run by force and coercion is doomed. To prevent man's destruction, one must grasp the principle: *Money is the root of all good.*

In the concrete sense, money is a commodity. It is the most marketable commodity, generally accepted and commonly used. It is acquired with the intention of later trading it. As a commodity, there can be too much or too little of it around. If there is too much in circulation, each unit is worth less. If there is too little money in circulation, each unit is worth more.

Money is a vehicle for economic calculation. It is the common denominator in all economic transactions. It functions as a medium of exchange. If men were to trade product for product, such as a basket of eggs for a pair of shoes, no money would be required. However, in advanced societies where men specialize in one field, primitive bartering is out of the question. Goods and services require a medium of exchange—money. Most goods and services are bought and sold against money—no goods, no money. Money means prices—no money, no prices. Money is worth only what it can buy.

Money should serve three functions. First, it is a means of payment. Money is used to pay bills, to buy and to sell goods and services. Second, it is a standard of value. The values of goods and services are quoted in terms of money. The resulting ratios are prices. Third, it is a store of value. It should retain its value until traded. Money should always be scarce; when it is not, it becomes a free good, devoid of value.

Good money must meet four requirements. It must be a commodity that possesses intrinsic value. Throughout history many mediums of exchange have been used and have had their shortcomings—cattle died; grain spoiled; human heads went out of vogue; silk ruined; logs awkward; spices spoiled; salt took too much; shells broke; feathers, furs, and whale teeth were not in steady supply.

The second requirement is that the commodity must not be too abundant, rendering it worthless, or too scarce, rendering it unattainable. It must have a steady supply to keep its value constant. Third, its worth must be easily recognized. It must be durable, portable, divisable and universally accepted. Finally, it must be independent of government decree. It must be accepted by choice. Ludwig von Mises observed that "the government is the only agency that can take a useful commodity like paper, slap some ink on it, and make it totally worthless." Fiat paper money is money of mere tokens which can neither be employed as a useful commodity nor redeemable into something of value. Money independent of government decree would nullify "legal tender" laws. No one would be forced to accept a less desirable commodity as money.

Around 700 B.C., as man emerged from the bartering stage of human life into the commercial stage, gold pellets were gaining acceptance as a medium of exchange. Since they differed in size, weight and fineness, they were awkward and time-consuming, for all pellets had to be graded for fineness and weighed for value. Perceiving this, Croesus, the clever King of Lydia, invented the coinage of gold.

With the help of coined gold money, Lydian producers and traders made their nation the foremost commercial success of the ancient world. The secret of that success was the powerful incentive furnished by gold coinage in preserving the fleeting energy of men by transformation into enduring gold. The gold would keep; the perishable products would spoil. Better have gold than spoiling products.[1]

---

[1]Theodore Macklin, "Short Changing Money," *California Mining Journal* (October, 1971), p. 9.

Evolution has eliminated most media of exchange. Gold and silver have remained. Gold has facilitated trade for thousands of years. Even today, knowledgeable citizens demand their government back the nation's currency with gold, and insist that the citizens be allowed to own gold, just in case the government tampers with the currency, rendering its value doubtful. As a medium of exchange, gold establishes trust between traders— be they individuals or governments. A lack of gold portends a breakdown in trade. A stable currency is a precondition to the division of labor. When workers are paid their worth in gold or a stable, gold-backed currency, work continues. All receive value for value. The stability of gold allows savings, and savings are the necessary means with which to plan for the future.

As a commodity, gold has intrinsic value; it is used for thousands of things—from measurement instrumentation to computers, from curing cancer and rheumatoid arthritis to transistors. It even protects astronauts from the blazing heat of the sun. In industry, it is one of the most useful metals. Gold is neither too abundant nor too scarce. Mines can produce a steady supply of it. The worth of a gold coin is easily recognizable because it is stamped directly on each coin. Bullion is stamped as to weight and fineness. Gold coins are practically indestructible; they cannot corrode, rust or tarnish. Gold coins can be easily moved—a little bit goes a long way; they can be carried off in an emergency and are accepted everywhere. Gold is easily worked into coins of small or large denominations or worked into jewelry. Finally, gold can be easily minted by private mints, independent of government decree. When it is free to trade side by side with government currency, the free market determines the value of each medium of exchange.

There is only one effective way to insure that money retains its value. Ideally, the money supply would expand and contract roughly in proportion to the expansion and contraction of goods and services exchanged, *independent* of any arbitrary manipulation by anyone. Where the quantity of money expands and contracts approximately in proportion to changes in the volume of goods and services transacted, this would be the automatic adjustment, and the general price level would remain substantially unchanged. The gold standard is the only system that has proven its ability to maintain stable prices, because over relatively short periods, it is similar to a fixed money supply, which keeps prices nearly fixed. Over relatively long periods of time, the gold standard system expands and contracts roughly in proportion to the long-term expansion in production, according to the vicissitudes of gold mining. And, most importantly, it is a system in which the volume of the money supply is *independent* of any arbitrary manipulation by anyone.

The Founding Fathers appreciated the value of gold and silver money. They fought hard and long to put an end to fiat paper money. To insure the use of gold and silver money by future generations, Article I, Section 8 of the Constitution gives Congress the power "to coin money," not to print it. In addition, Article I, Section 10 states: "No state shall . . . make anything but gold and silver coin a tender in payment of debts." The Founding Fathers understood that gold was money and money was gold, the best that could be had. It was one of the most important rights that they secured for future generations.

Gold is the ultimate form of money; it is not a managed money. It has no nationality; it is universally trusted and accepted. It is the universal standard for money and a store of value. Gold is treasured and honored throughout the world as the supreme standard of value. Whenever paper money falls in disrepute, people seek shelter for their wealth in gold. Gold is truly good money—the best form of money. It is out of the control of government; it is a refuge for citizens who mistrust the government; it allows financial transactions beyond the reach of the government. And, in the not too distant past, gold was for many the means of escape to freedom. In thousands of years of government propaganda, edicts, and confiscations, nothing has replaced gold; and it is doubtful that anything ever will.

5

WHAT IS CAPITALISM?

The gold standard springs eternally from freedom and succumbs to laws and regulations. Its implacable enemy is government in search of revenue. Whereas individuals produce goods and services in order to earn their living, government expropriates individual income and wealth in order to cover its expenses. Winston Churchill observed that the crime against society is not profit, but loss: "Private industry runs at a profit and uses the profit to expand producing capacity. Government industry runs at a loss and taxes the substance of the people to pay for its inefficiencies . . ."

The government's appetite for revenue is insatiable. That is why it is vital to understand that the purpose of the gold standard is to prevent government encroachment on private property. The gold standard works within the economic system. It is part of Capitalism.

The gold standard is not important as an isolated gadget but only as an integral part of a whole economic system. Just as "managed" paper money goes with a statist and collectivist philosophy, with government "planning," with a coercive economy in which the citizen is always at the mercy of bureaucratic caprice, so the gold standard is an integral part of a free-enterprise economy under which governments respect private property, economize in spending, balance their budgets, keep their promises, and refuse to connive in overexpansion of money or credit. . .[1]

---

[1]Henry Hazlitt, *What You Should Know About Inflation* (New York: D. Van Nostrand Company, Inc., 1965), pp. 26-27. Reprinted by permission of Van Nostrand Reinhold Company.

Since the gold standard is an integral part of the capitalistic system, and the capitalistic system engenders political and economic freedom, the study of capitalism is vital to the preservation of a free society.

Capitalism is the private ownership of the means of production. Capitalism is the only economic system that can uphold and protect individual rights. A controlled or managed economy is not based on individual rights, and cannot uphold and protect individual rights. Capitalism is the only moral economic system.

The case of the capitalistic economy versus the managed or planned economy has been on trial for the last two hundred years. It is the choice between the Declaration of Independence or the Communist Manifesto. It is the choice between freedom or slavery. The choice exists; it must be made. There is no kind of freedom and liberty other than the kind which the capitalistic economy develops.

With capitalism under constant attack in the schools and by pseudo-intellectuals, it is time to give it a fair trial. Understanding and appreciating economics is crucial to the maintenance of a free society. It should be the concern of every American. As conditions are today, nothing can be more important to every intelligent man than economics. His own future economic and physical health are at stake. For this reason the fundamental concepts of Capitalism are the subject of this chapter.

Capitalism is the life-blood of a free society. It is not a boring and unintelligible subject. It explains such wonders as: Who came first—the employer or the employee? Who runs the market —the producer or the consumer? How can more money buy less and why? And many, many more wonders that have been obfuscated by Keynesian economists, by socialist governments and by ignorant news media parroting both. The study of freedom and capitalism is stimulating, eye-opening, and exciting. For the man who never relaxes his search for truth, economics, especially Capitalism, is dynamic.

In eighteenth-century France the saying "laissez-faire" was the slogan of the champions of liberty. Their purpose was the establishment of the free market. In order to attain this end they advocated the abolition of all laws preventing more industrious and more efficient individuals from outdoing less industrious and less efficient competitors.

Laissez-faire means: Let each individual choose what he wants to do to cooperate in the division of labor; let the consumers determine what the entrepreneurs produce. Planning means: Let government alone choose and enforce its rulings by force and coercion. The question that must be decided is one of morality; which is right: Should man plan his own life, or should government plan it for him? It is individual freedom versus government omnipotence. Laissez-faire means: Let man choose and act; do not force him to yield to a dictator.[2]

Laissez-faire capitalism means a separation of state and economics, a totally unregulated and uncontrolled economy. It is free minds and a free market where trade is based on reason—no force or coercion. The free market is a series of unlimited, voluntary exchanges between traders for their own mutual benefit. As a result of the free price system, consumers' buying or abstention from buying channels production into those areas which are in demand by the consumer. The law of supply and demand works efficiently. Capitalism gives the economy sense and society functions orderly.

The essential role of government in a capitalistic society is to defend individual rights by protecting the nation and the marketplace. Every step it takes beyond that role, whether foreign or domestic, is a step toward a system of socialism where there is no freedom at all. In the marketplace, when government interferes or takes certain liberties, it is taking individual liberties out of the marketplace. Government forces the market to respond in a different way than the consumers would have wished. Liberty and freedom are the conditions of man within a contractual society. Meaning, that within the free market individuals are buyers or sellers by choice. Man works because he wants to be rewarded; he does not do compulsory labor nor does he pay

[2]Ludwig von Mises, *Human Action: A Treatise on Economics* (Chicago: Henry Regnery Company, 1963), p. 730.

tribute. He exchanges goods and services on the same basis. The buyer depends on the seller and the seller on the buyer. This is social cooperation in the division of labor. All receive value. Capitalism insures justice in the marketplace.

A basic requirement for the functioning of capitalism is a sound currency, a stable medium of exchange. When money continually depreciates, long-term contracts become unprofitable. It is important that the marketplace choose the best medium of exchange, one that will protect future profits. Free people usually choose gold and silver. When contracts are honored in gold, long-term planning is profitable. When workers are paid their worth in gold, silver or sound, gold-backed money, work continues, and the capitalistic system thrives.

Capitalism is the private ownership of the means of production. The function of the entrepreneur is to determine the employment of the factors of production. The owners of the means of production are capitalists and landowners. A capitalist, because he runs the risk of losing his capital, is also an entrepreneur and speculator. (A speculator is one who buys something in expectation of it rising in value. Nearly all Americans are speculators because there is no such thing as a safe investment; there are only degrees of safety.) The worker is concerned with changes in the labor market. Thus every function is integrated: the entrepreneur earns a profit or suffers a loss; the owners of the means of production (capital goods or land) earn interest; the workers earn wages.[3]

The entrepreneur is the driving force of the market. The direction of the market is the task of the entrepreneur. He controls production. He is at the helm and steers the ship. He is bound to obey unconditionally the captain's orders. The captain is the consumer.[4] The entrepreneur is driven by his own selfish interest in making profits and in acquiring wealth.

Profit is the key to capitalism. No one will risk his capital if there is no chance of a profit. Profit is the incentive to take

---

[3]*Ibid.*, p. 254.
[4]*Ibid.*, p. 269.

risks. No profit means no incentive; this can lead to a shortage of capital and a lack of progress. An economy will stagnate and eventually retrogress. To condemn profits is to increase losses and costs. To motivate the entrepreneur there must be profits. Income, wealth, and production are the results of thinking and action—employed by the entrepreneur for his profit.

In addition to serving as incentive for entrepreneurs and capitalists, profit performs a second important function. It allows savings and capital accumulation, which is the life-blood of an industrial society. It allows for improvement and creation of new plant and equipment. Efficient plant and equipment yield higher productivity. The higher the productivity, the higher the standard of living. The reason why the United States enjoys such a high standard of living is because the amount of invested capital per capita is greater than anywhere else in the world. Capital accumulation of profit is a prerequisite for a high standard of living.

Capitalism increases worker's real wage rates to the extent of reinvested capital. Savings and capital accumulation are an indispensable condition for technological improvement. Technology increases the output per unit of input, yielding higher productivity. "A tendency toward higher wage rates is not the cause, but the effect, of technological improvement."[5] The wages of workers in capitalistic countries far exceed those of non-capitalistic countries.

A high standard of living is the result of the production of more goods. Wealth is goods, something with intrinsic value, not paper money. One cannot buy prosperity with paper money; it must be created, i.e., produced. The effect of capitalism is continuing economic progress, a steady increase in the quantity of capital goods available at a lower price, and a continuous trend toward an improvement in the general standard of living.

When profits are high competition flourishes. Free competition rewards the best and most efficient producers. Competition keeps prices low. A business can corner a market only tem-

---

[5] *Ibid.*, p. 775.

porarily because high profits attract more competition. The corner is thus broken and prices are again competitive. "Antitrust" is a term used by government to mean government does not trust business. But the consumers certainly did; how else did small business grow into "big" business? To break up one, highly efficient company into several, small, less efficient companies, which by necessity must charge higher prices, is absurd. Business is built on mutual trust. Consumers' trust in a product earns business profits. Profits attract new capital and new businesses, competition flourishes, and monopolies are prevented; the one who benefits the most is the consumer. His money goes farther because prices are lower. (In a free market, monopolies can exist only as special privileges granted by government.)

The consumer is captain of the economy. Profit and loss are the devices by which he exercises his supremacy on the market. Profit tells the entrepreneur that the consumer approves of his action; loss, that he disapproves. By his buying or abstention from buying, the consumer determines what should be produced, in what quantity and in what quality. The consumer determines which producer will succeed and which will fail; he makes rich men poor and poor men rich. (If not the consumer, then the government.) The producer must comply with the wishes of the consumer. The market is inescapable; it is the supreme law. The market stops losses by withdrawing the factors of production from the inefficient, who by necessity charge higher prices, and transfers them to the efficient producer, whose prices are lower. The market checks losses and eliminates waste. In the form of lower prices, the consumer again benefits.

Another important function of the free market is the division of labor. In a free market all those who want to work can find work. The market wage rate tends toward a level at which all those eager to earn wages get jobs and all those eager to employ workers hire as many as they want. It tends toward full employment. On the labor market there are buyers for every supply of labor offered. There can be abundance in only segments of the labor market; it results in pushing labor to other segments and thereby increasing production in that segment of the economy.

Under capitalism there is no mass unemployment. Unemployment is a result of government interference in the economy either by minimum wage laws which fix the wage rates at a higher point than the free market's prevailing rate or by allowing unions to force up wage rates. Institutional unemployment has become a chronic or permanent mass phenomenon since government legislated minimum wage laws, full employment laws, and gave unions the power to force up wage rates. These are characteristics of government interference in the free market, not an effect of capitalism.

The benefits from capitalism have been nothing less than remarkable. Its driving force, the profit-motive, forces the businessman to constantly provide the consumers with more, better and cheaper products. Directed by the most energetic, far-sighted individuals, it results in mass production for mass consumption.

The laissez-faire ideology laid the groundwork for the Industrial Revolution. It blasted apart the system of castes, guilds and monopolies that had restricted and prohibited competition. It wiped out slavery by the great liberator—the industrialist. It demolished the social order in which a constantly increasing number of people were doomed to abject need and destitution. The outstanding fact about the Industrial Revolution is that it opened an age of mass production for the needs of the masses. The wage earners were no longer working for other people's well-being. They themselves were the main consumers of the products from the factories. (Contrary to popular opinion, the only economic system that can raise the standard of living of the poor is capitalism.) People thronged to the factories as the only way to improve their standard of living. As low as the wages were, they were a means of survival. The industrialists did not and could not force anyone to work in their factories. Women, who had no food to feed their children, and children, who were destitute and starving, fled to the factories. It was their only refuge. "It saved them, in the strict sense of the term, from death by starvation."[6]

Capitalism created the greatest environment of freedom known

---

[6]*Ibid.*, p. 620.

to man. It produced geniuses, men who pioneered in the arts and sciences. It raised the standard of living to unprecedented heights. It gave the world nearly one hundred years of peace. It has proven that man, when allowed to live by reason and to plan his own life, will create and produce in order to improve his standard of living.

Man, by choice, is moral. He lives for his own interest, not as a sacrificial animal for the benefit of government or society. Reasoning, creating man can only exist in a free society.

If they understood its true meaning, Americans would be proud to wear the title "Capitalists." That tells the world that one comes from a country where men are free—free to think, to plan, to act, to keep the fruits of their labor—a country that upholds and protects individual rights. That tells the world that one lives under the only moral economic system—Capitalism.

6

WHAT IS SOCIALISM?

Socialism is not new. It grew and developed in the nineteenth century. By the turn of the twentieth century an immense majority of many countries were already radical supporters of socialism. The Germans were firmly committed to the principles of Nazism—the German National *Socialist* Labor Party, where the common welfare ranked above private profit; "profit-seeking business harms the vital interest of the immense majority and that it is the sacred duty of popular government to prevent the emergence of profits by public control of production and distribution."[1] The Italians were more fanatical in their support of socialism. The Italian socialists named their party the Fascists. Fascism and Nazism were *socialist* dictatorships. Lenin had the grandest plan of all. He chose as the official name for his government—Union of the Soviet *Socialist* Republics. No reference to Russia or to the communists was made. He designed a name that would encompass the "socializing" of all countries. By the time the 1930s had arrived so had the American New Deal. Socialism had found its way across the Atlantic.

The characteristic mark of this age of dictators, wars, revolutions, and inflation is socialism. Socialism is the opposite of capitalism. Socialism is a social system based on public ownership of the means of production. All material resources, including labor, are owned and operated by the government. The government is the sole employer, and no one has an opportunity to own more property or to better himself over and above what government allots to him.

Because socialism is the enemy of capitalism and it is being supported by Americans as the wave of the future, or at least

---

[1] Ludwig von Mises, *Planned Chaos* (New York: The Foundation for Economic Education, Inc., 1947), p. 75.

the inevitable system of the future, Americans should have an opportunity to judge if they really want to switch allegiance to socialism. This chapter studies socialism and the paragon of socialism—the U.S.S.R.

Not realizing that their methods are socialistic, most governments, political parties, and labor unions are eager to restrict the sphere of private initiative and free enterprise. They have forgotten that capitalism is thriving in spite of their measures. They are preoccupied with the social aspects of things, with government omnipotence and government measures. They expect everything from authoritarian action and very little from the initiative of enterprising citizens. They ignore the fact that the unprecedented and unparalleled achievements of the United States were the result of private enterprise. The United States was founded by individual citizens using their own initiative, intellect, and courage long before government established itself as overseer.

Capitalism, i.e., the free market, is generally unpopular today, and all of society's problems are charged to it. Socialism, some say, is much fairer. These advocates of socialism can be divided into two groups. One group wants to improve capitalism by government interference with the market. They are called interventionists. They want to substitute a mixed economy—halfway between capitalism and socialism. The other group wants to use interventionism as a stepping-stone to full socialism. The difference between interventionism and socialism is in name only.

Socialism is the establishment of a bureaucracy-run economy. All economic enterprises are departments of the government. The whole nation forms one single labor army with compulsory service; the commander of this army is the chief of state. Under interventionism the means of production remain privately owned. Although it appears as capitalism, it is socialism. Government fixes prices, wages, and interest rates. Government decrees at what wages laborers should work and for whom. The central board of production management is supreme. The economy is directed by economic czars. All citizens are merely civil servants. It is still a market economy, however. The government seeks to influence the market by intervention of its coercive power, but it does not want to eliminate the market altogether.

Nonetheless, all the methods of interventionism are doomed to failure. In their quest to help the market via minimum wage rates, government-created jobs, taxation, and credit expansion, they are actually sabotaging it. With the excuse that their controls and regulations are insufficient to solve all the problems, they demand more power to solve the very problems that they created in the first place. In the end, the market economy is replaced by bureaucracies, and interventionism turns into socialism. Interventionism results in disaster and chaos.

Most interventionists are driven by an envious resentment against those whose incomes are larger than their own. The existence of profits is objectionable to them. They speak of profit without dealing with its corollary, loss. Americans, however, do not fear nor are they envious of profits and successful businessmen. In fact, they admire and respect success. Americans basically distrust those who downgrade "materialism," because materialism stands for a desire to achieve wealth, which implies a desire to achieve values, i.e., to think, to act, to be independent. If Americans were presented with a clear-cut choice between capitalism and socialism, socialism would be thrown out. (For further proof see the 1972 presidential election results.) Socialism is an alien philosophy; if it continues to dominate the thinking in the United States, it will destroy America's immense wealth and basically free society.

Some interventionists are shocked when confronted with the realism that their policies foster dictatorial tendencies and lead to totalitarian socialism. They sincerely believe they can create a fairer distribution of income. They fail to realize that the various measures they suggest are incapable of producing the results they desire, and will produce a state of affairs which is worse than the previous one.

To illustrate, the following example is an analysis of a typical case of price control. It deals with the milk industry.

If the government wants to make it possible for poor parents to give milk to their children, it must buy milk at the market price and sell it to those poor people with a loss at a cheaper rate; the loss may be covered from the means collected by taxation. But if the government simply fixes the price of milk at a lower rate than the market, the results obtained will be contrary to the aims of the government. The marginal producers will, in order to avoid losses, go out of the business of producing and selling milk. There will be less milk available for the consumers, not more. This outcome is contrary to the government's intentions. The government interfered because it considered milk as a vital necessity. It did not want to restrict its supply.

Now the government has to face the alternative: either to refrain from any endeavors to control prices or to add to its first measure a second one, i.e., to fix the prices of the factors of production necessary for the production of milk . . . Thus the government has to go further and further, fixing the prices of all the factors of production both human (labor) and material. . . .

But when this state of all-round control of business is achieved, the market economy has been replaced by a system of planned economy, by socialism. . . .[2]

If the government, faced with its first failure, does not return to a free economy, it must keep adding more and more regulations and restrictions. In this way it proceeds to a point in which all economic freedom of individuals has disappeared. In the end there is only socialism.

The waste and suffering that socialism produces are unnecessary. Free enterprise is much more efficient. Besides, Americans know there is no such thing as a "free lunch." They want to work for a living. They thrive on competition. They want no government favors, handouts, or charity. They can and have survived on their own initiative for over two hundred years. Government favors and special privileges are relics of the age of kings and czars. Americans want to succeed by their own effort and ability. They have what it takes to make it on their own. The whole

---

[2]*Ibid.*, pp. 23-24.

consideration of socialism is repulsive to the American way of life.

What it boils down to when socialists talk about raising farm prices, raising wage rates, or lowering profits, ultimately refers to the government forcing these changes on the free market. Yet the authors of these projects insist that they are planning for freedom. This program of self-contradictory interventionism is dictatorship, supposedly to make people free. But the liberty its supporters advocate is liberty to do the things that they themselves want to be done.

There can be no freedom to live where one chooses when government decides where one works. There can be no freedom to choose the career one wants when government is the sole employer and assigns everyone a job he must perform. There can be no freedom of thought or action when government has the power to remove opposition, permanently. Within a socialist society, there is no room left for freedom.

The meanings of the words socialism and communism are synonymous. Russia is named the Union of Soviet *Socialist* (not Communist) Republics.

Americans can be proud of the fact that when Lenin was recruiting communists, he failed in America. He realized the workers lacked the revolutionary spirit because they had already achieved well-being and were too busy making money. It is a communist trick to incite envy in those with lower incomes against all those with higher incomes. Capitalism, by raising the incomes of everyone, creates peace, not social unrest.

Communists have their own way of quelling social unrest. Their idea of all-round planning results in dictatorship. In advocating dictatorship such people always advocate the dictatorship of their own group. In advocating planning such people always have in mind their own plan, not that of others. They will never admit that a socialist or communist regime is true and genuine socialism or communism if it does not assign to them the most eminent position and the highest income. The essential feature of genuine communism is that all affairs are precisely conducted according to their own will and that all those who disagree are beaten into submission. Dictatorships and violent oppression of all dissenters are today exclusively socialist institutions.

Setting aside the political repulsiveness of socialism, for a moment, here is an illustration of the economic impossibility of socialism. The following commentary is taken from an editorial prepared by Alexander Sachs, internationally known economic adviser and industrial consultant, which appeared in the November 6, 1972, issue of *Barrons*. It was entitled "Desperate State—Disaster in Soviet Agriculture is Largely Man-Made."

The big Russian wheat deal that was consummated in the summer of 1972 was necessary, according to prevailing opinions, because of that year's Soviet crop disaster, which chiefly sprang from adverse weather conditions. While this has been a traditional excuse for disappointing harvests, the truth of the matter, according to Mr. Sachs, was the Soviet *socialized* and *collectivized* economic system.

For instance, the Soviet fire-fighting apparatus was seriously inadequate. The Soviets proved unable to cope with vast forest fires, which subsequently led to the evacuation of whole villages and the total loss of their crops. In the Asian regions, at other critical junctures, freight cars fell short of need, tractors and harvest machinery proved inoperative for lack of spare parts, trucks arrived minus vital parts, which, presumably, were stolen en route to meet deficiencies elsewhere.

Grain imports were being jammed by bad organization, noncooperation between railwaymen and port authorities, and a shortage of boxcars. Railroad management in the first half of October delivered only forty-one per cent of the freight cars needed to move the grain. The cars eventually used were unsuitable, spilling grain along the tracks. It took longer to process the documents than to load the grain. This illustrated both the shortage of technical facilities and bureaucratic incompetence.

Mr. Sachs concluded, we are not dealing with a crisis predominately caused by bad weather, but with a more fundamental malignancy that is inherent in the Soviet system and its pattern of farming. State and collective farming has produced an agriculture hopelessly mired in sociological prejudice and isolated from factory and laboratory. The truly desperate state of the Soviet farm economy relates back to the Five-Year Plan. It is the very existence of such a Plan, contended Mr. Sachs, principally designed for the command-type of industrial production and burgeoning arms industry, that hobbles the progress of Russian agriculture. Rooted in their economic administration are a hereditary class of political careerists. It is the sons and daughters (and now the grandchildren) of revolutionary leaders from whom the staff of economic administrators and planners is recruited. Loyalty to the party is the major requisite for industrial and farm management. Thus there is a permanent bar to advancement by ability. The revolution of 1917 and the collectivization of agriculture effectively aborted farm modernization and industrialization of the USSR.

All civilizations have up to now been based on private property. As the Soviet regime proves, only nations committed to the principle of private property have risen above poverty and produced science, art, and literature. There is no experience to show that any other social system could provide mankind with any of the achievements of civilization.

The fundamental objection against socialism is that in a truly socialist regime money is not used. There are no market prices for the factors of production since they are neither bought nor sold; it is impossible to resort to calculation in planning future action and in determining the result of past action. A socialist management of production would squander the scarce factors of production both material and human, (labor). Chaos and poverty for all would unavoidably result.

The second main objection against socialism is that it is a less efficient mode of production than is capitalism. In a socialist society the standard of living of the majority of the people will be low when compared with conditions prevailing under capitalism. If the Soviet regime were regarded as an experiment, the result has clearly demonstrated the superiority of capitalism and the inferiority of socialism.

An argument persued by many socialists is that the United States has achieved so much affluence because of her immense natural resources, not her capitalistic economic system. But the facts do not bear this out. Russia's "soil is much better endowed by nature than that of any other nation. It offers the most advantageous conditions for the growing of all kinds of cereals, fruits, seeds and plants. Russia owns immense pastures and almost inexhaustible forests. It has the richest resources for the production of gold, silver, platinum, iron, copper, nickel, manganese and all other metals and of oil."[3] It is not what a country has, but how it exploits what it has. But for the despotism of the Czars and the lamentable inefficiency of the socialist system, Russia could have long ago enjoyed the highest standard of living.

There is a basic conflict between capitalism and socialism. In this conflict everybody must take a stand. Either one is for economic freedom or one is for totalitarian socialism. There is no middle-of-the-road position, namely interventionism. Freedom is freedom—one cannot be part free and part slave. There is no such thing as "excessive" economic freedom. It is up to each individual to choose between the market economy and socialism. Government can preserve the market economy solely by respecting private property, or it can control the market through the means of production. Society is run either by the consumers by means of supply and demand in the free market, or by the government by force and coercion.

Freedom and liberty always mean freedom from government interference. The irreconcilable conflict between rule of law versus rule of men (force), has been man's history with man. It was a long and hard evolution. The rule of law, or limited government, as safeguarded by the Constitution and the Bill of Rights, is the characteristic mark of the paragon of capitalism— the United States of America.

But freedom of life, liberty, and property is a sham in a country in which economic freedom is prohibited. There must first be respect for private property before there is respect for other individual rights, such as, due process of law, and the right to be secure against unreasonable search and seizure. These

---

[3]*Ibid.*, p. 48.

rights are a sham if government is allowed to seize private property without due process of law to satisfy a tax liability. No other creditor has that right. Trotsky summarized the socialist economic system concisely: "In a country where the sole employer is the State, opposition means death by slow starvation. The old principle: who does not work shall not eat, has been replaced by a new one: who does not obey shall not eat."

What the socialist experience in Russia proves beyond a doubt is that it results in a very low standard of living for the majority of the people and unlimited dictatorial despotism. If it were not for massive aid from the United States government, a Russian revolution probably would have freed her people long ago.

Socialism has conquered three-quarters of the people in the world because it has rarely and ineffectively been opposed. The policy of appeasement (as with Hitler) has been practiced universally for many decades. It is this complacency that makes some people believe the coming of socialism is inevitable. But this is untrue. The majority of people do not resist socialism because they trust the socialist propaganda that bombards the news media and educational institutions. Capitalism only leads to socialism when government is encouraged to interfere in the economy and thus bring about socialism.

The coming of socialism is far from inevitable. As Thomas Jefferson once declared: "An elective despotism was not the government we fought for." He warned that the only defense against tyranny is an informed electorate. It takes intellectual and moral courage to seek the truth. That is what it will take to reverse the trend toward socialism and pave the way back to freedom. Reason and ideas determine the course of man's future. It is not enough to fight an evil. One must want to achieve, to fight for, a good. What is needed to stop the trend toward socialism and tyranny is the open and unrestricted recognition and support of capitalism.

7

CAPITALISM VS. SOCIALISM

The antithesis of capitalism is socialism. All socialist societies are fundamentally the same. The basic value of a socialist society is death, as opposed to life in a capitalistic society. Socialism condemns the idea that man possesses inalienable rights to life, liberty, and pursuit of happiness. The basic premise of man's morality is changed from man is an end in himself, to the premise that man does not live for his own sake, but for the sake of others, happiness on earth is impossible, and the pursuit of happiness is futile. This is the philosophy of Altruism, of self-sacrifice, which destroys all standards, values, incentives, and ultimately, life itself. Its political corollary is dictatorship. Its economic corollary is socialism.

Under socialism the state is considered omnipotent and omniscient; it is supreme. There are no individual rights; the rights to life, liberty, and happiness are denied. There are no property rights. And beyond the sphere of private property and the free market lies the sphere of force and coercion. Individual freedom is denied. The only right allowed, because it cannot be denied, is the right to commit suicide. Since capitalism is the only moral economic system because it respects individual rights and guarantees individual freedom, socialism is an immoral system because it denies individual rights and prohibits individual freedom. A man with no freedom is a slave. Philosophically, the choice between capitalism versus socialism is really a choice between freedom versus slavery.

Socialism promises that if men will give up their individual rights to the state, the state will see to it that all men will be equal—there will be continual bliss and prosperity. Man will be free from want; he will be secure. The state will take care of all the people.

43

Another word employed to mean equal is egalitarianism. Socialists use it to mean not equality before the law (which already exists in the United States), but to mean inequality: the establishment of a new society, with a new set of standards— equality and prosperity for the chosen few.

The egalitarians and the altruists are today's barbarians invading man's right to life, liberty and the pursuit of happiness. They say that they want to "liberate" mankind. But what the socialists really want is liberation from reality, from the fact that $A = A$ and causes have effects. If they really wanted freedom, equality, and prosperity for all, they would be fighting for capitalism, which protects the freedom, the rewards and the incentives for every individual's achievement, each to the extent of his ability and ambition, thus raising the intellectual, moral, and economic state of the whole society.

This chapter will prove that socialism produces not prosperity, but poverty, not security but insecurity. It will show how socialists try to subvert and undermine capitalistic societies, always with the excuse of "taking care" of the people.

Socialism produces poverty, hunger, and death, nothing else. All promises to the contrary are lies. No government can manage an economy successfully. There are three reasons: first, no individual or government is omnipotent and/or omniscient; second, the purpose of the socialist government is to create stability, when in reality there exists no stability; nothing is perpetual but change; third, it is impossible to satisfy all the consumers' demands. For example, in a constantly changing world, man makes hundreds of thousands of decisions in his lifetime—some simple, some complex; some right, some wrong. No group of men can possibly choose the right answer for thousands of decisions for millions of people. If it were possible man would have created paradise long ago. Another way to look at it is, if running a business is so easy, then why are there so few millionaires?

Competition is the only way to meet consumer demands. Competition enables the businessman to constantly check his premises against those of his competition to see whether his idea really works. If it does not, then either he goes bankrupt or, if he is clever, he will change his idea and go on to meet the competition's challenge. Under socialism there is no competition to regulate government. No plan that government ever puts into operation can be tested by a competitor. This means that an error in government planning is almost never corrected, except by depression, revolution, or war[1]—measures too costly to show that government was wrong. Free enterprise is exceptionally more efficient.

By prohibiting the free market and the profit-motive, socialism tries to escape from reality, from thinking and action. It forces all men to suffer with a lower standard of living. True, all men are economically equal—but they are equally poor. The standard of success is the lowest common denominator. None are "permitted" to rise above the lowest level. The exception, and there is always one under socialism, is the elite—the ruling class. Those few men who lie, cheat, and murder to reach the top, who have the "superior wisdom" by which they run the economy, are granted special privileges. But the majority of the people live in fear under a constant reign of terror. They are poor, starving, and miserable human beings.

The foremost tool that socialist governments use to gain control over an economy and over the people is the banking system. In fact, the fifth plank of Karl Marx's Communist Manifesto reads: "Centralization of credit in the hands of the state, by means of a national bank with state capital and an exclusive monopoly." Lenin said that the establishment of a central bank is ninety per cent of communizing a country. This is underscored by the observation of Reginald McKenna, President of the Midlands Bank of England: "Those that create and issue the money and credit direct the policies of government and hold in their hands the destiny of the people." Amachel Rothschild was quoted as saying: "Give me the power to issue a nation's money; then I do not care who makes the laws." The Founding Fathers were aware of the threat of a central bank. Thomas Jefferson

---

[1]Harry D. Schultz, *Panics and Crashes and How You Can Make Money Out of Them* (New York: Arlington House, 1972), p. 149.

wrote to John Adams: ". . . I sincerely believe, with you, that banking establishments are more dangerous than standing armies . . ." President Andrew Jackson on July 10, 1832, stated that the Bank of the United States, was "unauthorized by the Constitution, subversive of the rights of the States, and dangerous to the liberties of the people." Then he abolished the bank.

But as a result of a series of economic disasters,[2] Congress passed the Federal Reserve Act of 1913. This act was to eliminate economic disasters in the future. It promised that there would be no more boom and bust cycles, only steady growth and perpetual prosperity. Sound familiar? The Federal Reserve Act nationalized the banking system of the United States.

Since the establishment of the Federal Reserve Act in 1913, eight recessions have been created and the United States has experienced its worst depression and its worst inflation in modern times. Since Woodrow Wilson took his oath of office the national debt has risen from $1 billion to $450 billion. The gold supply is mortgaged seven times over and the silver has all been sold. The treasury has been looted.

The Federal Reserve was created precisely because only a free banking system can keep credit expansion and government expansion within narrow limits and only a free banking system can secure the economy against crises and depressions.

When the tremendous economic and political power of money was recognized, its issuance and control were seized everywhere as a government monopoly. The banking system in the United States is not part of the capitalistic system. Government holds a monopoly over the issuance of money and credit. This is the strongest and hardest monopoly to break up, but it must be done.

The Federal Reserve is so powerful that Congressman Wright Patman, Chairman of the House Banking Committee, maintains: "In the United States today we have in effect two governments. . . We have the duly constituted Government. . . Then we have an independent, uncontrolled and uncoordinated government in the

---

[2]Gary Allen, *None Dare Call It Conspiracy* (California: Concord Press, 1971), pp. 43-45.

Federal Reserve System, operating the money powers which are reserved to Congress by the Constitution." In its sixty-year history, the Federal Reserve has never been audited. The Federal Reserve handles hundreds of billions of dollars of government and individual money, and its books have never been audited by government officials since the organization came into existence. Since 1964, Chairman Patman has been trying to persuade Federal Reserve officials into "permitting" a government audit.

The Federal Reserve did not delude all Congressmen. Congressman Charles A. Lindbergh, Sr., father of the famous aviator, told Congress: "This act establishes the most gigantic trust on earth. . . The new law will create inflation whenever the trusts want inflation." Henry Cabot Lodge, Sr., proclaimed: "The bill as it stands seems to me to open the way to a vast inflation of the currency. . . I do not like to think that any law can be passed which will make it possible to submerge the gold standard in a flood of irredeemable paper money." (*Congressional Record*, June 10, 1932.)

In 1933, President Roosevelt with one stroke of the pen, confiscated the gold holdings of all United States citizens, abolished the classical gold standard, devalued the dollar, and ushered in a new era of American government—the age of American socialism had begun.

Once the banking system is under control, manipulation of the money supply and credit begins. The form it takes is inflation. Inflation is caused by an increase in the supply of money and credit. As more money is printed, the value of each existing unit decreases. Goods rise in price, not because goods are scarcer than before, but because money is more abundant. Because people have more money, each unit is valued less. Inflation is currency debasement and currency depreciation. It is government-created; it is a hidden tax on the unsuspecting citizen. Since government controls the money supply, credit expansion is exclusively a government practice.

Keynesian economists promise that credit expansion will produce plenty of capital goods, lower interest rates, lavish government spending, full employment, redistribution of the wealth by expropriating the wealth of the capitalists, everlasting booms, and make everybody prosperous. This is nonsense. The implications of such promises are contrary to the promises themselves. When Keynesians promise to make everybody prosperous by increasing "credit," they are saying that the way to prosperity is to increase debt. When they promise full employment by increasing wage rates, they are saying that the way to full employment is to increase costs of production. When they promise to increase the national wealth by paying out government subsidies, they are saying that the way to national wealth is to increase taxes.[3]

Lord Keynes was a charlatan. His economic philosophy has bankrupted the United States. As a socialist, Keynes promised something for nothing—a promise that bureaucrats could not pass up. Honest men, however, do not fake reality—they produce what they want.

Inflation is one of the most underhanded, conniving schemes to which politicians resort. Politicians, says Henry Hazlitt, "talk of inflation as if it were some horrible visitation from without, over which they had no control—like a flood, a foreign invasion, or a plague. . . Yet the truth is that political leaders bring on inflation by their own monetary and fiscal policies."[4]

Here is how it works:

Let us assume that the government issues an additional quantity of paper money. The government plans either to buy commodities and services or to repay debts incurred or to pay interest on such debts. However this may be, the treasury enters the market with an additional demand for goods and services; it is now in a position to buy more goods than it could buy before. The prices of the commodities it buys rise. If the government had expended in its purchases money collected by taxation, the taxpayers would have re-

---

[3]Henry Hazlitt, *Economics in One Lesson* (New York: Harper & Row, Publishers, 1946), pp. 213-14.

[4]Henry Hazlitt, *What You Should Know About Inflation*, p. 1.

stricted their purchases and, while the prices of goods bought by the government would have risen, those of other goods would have dropped. But this fall in the prices of goods the taxpayers used to buy does not occur if the government increases the quantity of money at its disposal without reducing the quantity of money in the hands of the public. The prices of some commodities—viz., of those the government buys —rise immediately, while those of the other commodities remain unaltered for the time being. But the process goes on. Those selling the commodities asked for by the government are now themselves in a position to buy more than they used previously. The prices of the things these people are buying in larger quantities therefore rise too. Thus the boom spreads from one group of commodities and services to other groups until all prices and wage rates have risen. The rise in prices is thus not synchronous for the various commodities and services.[5]

The boom can last only as long as the credit expansion progresses at an ever accelerated pace. When the public finally wakes up, it suddenly realizes that inflation is a deliberate policy and prices will go up endlessly. The ultimate reaction of the public is the "flight into real values"; they frantically exchange paper money for goods in an attempt to salvage some of their capital. Within a very short time, weeks or days, the paper money that was used as a medium of exchange is no longer acceptable. It has become worthless. This is the crack-up boom and the complete breakdown of the whole monetary system. Inflation cannot be a permanent policy because, when continued, it must finally result in a complete annihilation of the currency.

The results of inflation are disastrous to the market, to the economy, and most of all, to the individual. Inflationary policies result in overconsumption and malinvestment. False prosperity leads to obsolete and useless plant and equipment. Capital is wasted; the market is impaired. Debtors are favored at the expense

---

[5]Mises, *Human Action,* p. 412.

of creditors. The wealth of various individuals has been affected differently. Some are enriched, some impoverished. Inflation makes it possible for some people to get rich by speculation and windfall instead of by hard work. Saving is discouraged and extravagance encouraged. People on fixed incomes are hurt the most. It rewards gambling and penalizes thrift. It promotes squandering, envy, resentment, corruption, crime, and an increasing drift toward more intervention which may end in dictatorship.

The public is morally ravaged. They are despondent and dispirited. The more optimistic they were under the illusory prosperity of the boom, the greater is their despair and their feeling of frustration. Their trusted officials have just robbed them of their earnings and savings. And the blame is placed on the people or on speculators instead of the real culprit—government. The final outcome of credit expansion is general impoverishment. The government, meanwhile, has used this immoral act for its own expansion, to become more totalitarian and seemingly more efficient.

In the hands of socialists inflation is a lethal weapon. It enables government to bleed a country, expand its power and demoralize its people. The history of the ravages of inflation is a gruesome one indeed. The German hyper-inflation of 1922-23 paved the way for Hitler. The hyper-inflation in China after World War II paved the way for Mao Tse-tung. And herein lies the insidious threat of inflation. It seems the chances of a country staying free after hyper-inflation are very small indeed.

Henry Hazlitt maintains that if the welfarist-socialist-inflationist trend of recent years continues in this country, the outlook is dark. It is a prospect of mounting taxation, snowballing expenditures, chronic deficits, a budget out of control, an accelerating rate of inflation of the kind endemic in Latin America (at least for the last generation), a collapse of the dollar, increasing world currency chaos, and more and more ruthless price, wage, and exchange controls, leading toward a regimented economy and dictatorship. And if this trend is interrupted temporarily, it may be by riots, assassinations, and a breakdown of law and order.[6]

When the inflationary boom ceases, the currency has been destroyed and business ruined. Depression sets in. This is the boom and bust cycle, produced not by capitalism, but by socialist inflationary policy.

A depression is a necessary although unpleasant process by which an economy adjusts, throws off the excesses and distortions of the previous inflationary boom, and reestablishes a sound economic condition. The sooner the depression-readjustment is gotten over with, the better. But socialists use this period to blame capitalism for the depression and to add more controls to their stranglehold on the economy. By trying to lend money to unsound business, prop up wage rates and consumer prices, or reinflate, government prolongs the agony and converts a sharp, quick depression into a lingering, chronic disease. This perpetual depression causes mass unemployment, additional suffering, and further demoralization of the people.

Ludwig von Mises asserts that economics recommends neither inflationary nor deflationary policy. It does not urge government to tamper with the market's choice of a medium of exchange. It establishes only the following truths:

1. By committing itself to an inflationary or deflationary policy a government does not promote the public welfare . . . or the interests of the whole nation. It merely favors one or several groups of the population at the expense of the other groups.

2. It is impossible to know in advance which group will be favored by a definite inflationary or deflationary measure and to what extent . . .

3. . . . a monetary expansion results in misinvestment of capital and overconsumption. It leaves the nation as a whole poorer, not richer . . .

---

[6]Henry Hazlitt, *Man Vs. the Welfare State* (New York: Arlington House, 1969), p. 215.

4. Continued inflation must finally end in the crack-up boom, the complete breakdown of the currency system.

5. Deflationary policy is costly for the treasury and unpopular with the masses. But inflationary policy is a boon for the treasury and very popular with the ignorant. Practically, the danger of deflation is but slight and the danger of inflation tremendous.[7]

In addition to the inflation-depression method to undermine capitalism, socialists employ taxation. The progressive income tax is the second plank in the *Communist Manifesto*. Taxes are collected by a branch of government, which uses fear, intimidation, and "Gestapo" measures to force people to part with their property.

The effects of taxation are more easily discernible than those of inflation: taxes basically take from one group to give to another group—rob Peter to pay Paul. Taxation is a form of expropriation of the successful producers, who are thus penalized. The incentive to keep producing is removed, since the more a man produces, the larger is his tax burden. Taxation limits competition because new businesses cannot acquire wealth to expand and become big business. Old established businesses are privileged by the tax system. Progressive taxation checks economic progress, consumers' demands are defied and the economy generally stagnates.

The high level and the complexities of the personal income tax reward the dishonest and those with government influence but burden the honest without influence. Both the government and the people are corrupted.

Private property and confiscatory measures are incompatible. Since taxation prevents capital accumulation and savings, which are essential to capitalism, taxes destroy capitalism. As Chief Justice Marshall observed, the power to tax, is the power to destroy.

It is argued that taxes are necessary to support the services of

---

[7]Mises, *Human Action*, pp. 470-71.

government. It is claimed that without government regulation utilities would not function for the benefit of all the people, telephone service would become inefficient, postal service would become too costly, and the railroads would not serve all those who wanted service. It is argued that public utilities should be run by the government for the public. The truth is that since government has interfered with private enterprise in the oil and gas industry, for instance, there have been shortages, higher prices, work stoppage because of lack of fuel which closed plants, cold homes, and rotting food because the grain could not be processed since the machines lacked fuel. Telephone service is crumbling under government price controls. The postal service runs at a deficit (at taxpayer's expense) every year and theft has become a major problem. The railroads are going bankrupt. In short, the public is paying for service not received. And the industries that are not controlled have managed to serve the public exceptionally well: the shoe industry, the food industry, and the construction industry, to name a few. Taxes do not produce benefits which the taxpayer would have otherwise missed.

Taxation is another way in which socialist governments betray their citizens. The servant becomes master. There is no stopping high taxation, which an expanding government requires, unless government spending, and, of course, government expanding, stops. Socialism is financed by heavy taxation while at the same time it intentionally destroys the free market. In fighting profits through taxation, governments deliberately sabotage the free market, private property, and individual liberty.

Other socialist measures are government subsidies, tariffs, nationalization, and minimum wage laws. Subsidies and tariffs benefit one group at the expense of another group. Government employs them with the excuse that they are helping out a vital industry. This is impossible, because a basic lesson regarding capitalism is:

When a capitalistic economy faces problems, it must face them with capitalistic measures—that is, increase the flow of capital spending (not government spending). Capitalistic problems cannot be cured with socialistic remedies. Only in a pure socialistic economy will socialistic measures, such as increased government spending and increased taxes, serve to relieve the problems. Experience indicates that even in socialistic societies, the device of government spending does not cure—it merely relieves the condition temporarily.[8]

When it comes to running a business, the same holds true for government as for the individual: it has no more ability to create something out of nothing. Government cannot run a business at a loss or subsidize an unprofitable project unless it withdraws the means from taxpayers by taxation. When the government spends more, taxpayers spend less. The public pays for public works. When there is no profit-motive, responsibility is drowned among bureaucratic rules and regulations. The results of centralization and nationalization policies are political corruption, poor service and financial failure.

Minimum wage laws are a good example of the subversive effect of government interference. In a free market all those who want to work and those who want to employ workers are able to meet their needs. When government decides that the lower wage earner's earnings are too low and passes legislation to increase his earnings, it raises the wage rate level above the free market wage rate level. Business being business, jobs are reduced by the rise in costs. The higher the minimum wage, the higher the unemployment. It distorts the whole wage picture. In the long run everybody's earnings go up proportionately; and who foots the bill? The consumer pays more for the same product. Thus, minimum wage laws cause chronic unemployment and higher costs—a result of government interference in the free market—a socialist characteristic.

The Federal Reserve Act, prohibition of gold ownership, inflation, taxation, nationalization, and minimum wage laws are

---

[8]Donald I. Rogers, *How to Beat Inflation by Using It* (New York: Arlington House, 1970), p. 85.

inherent ways that socialists undermine capitalism and freedom. They all involve the same principle: government's disrespect for private property (the free market).

These programs have been tolerated and even encouraged because some people are under the misunderstanding that it is the function of government or the right of government to expropriate the wealth of the privileged and distribute it among the underprivileged. This is called the "fair" redistribution of the national income. The premise here to be questioned is: Since some people appropriate to themselves more than they should, the portions of other people are curtailed. The answer is, first, an intrinsic feature of capitalism is that the wealth is owned unevenly. Nikolai Lenin appreciated this fact when he observed that "uneven economic and political development is an absolute law of Capitalism." Second, it is nonsensical to try to figure the national income or national wealth. An individual can convert his property into money, but a nation cannot. Third, within a capitalistic economy goods are not first produced, appropriated, and then distributed. There is no such thing as the appropriation of ownerless goods. Goods come into existence as somebody's property. If one wants to distribute them, one must first confiscate them. Therefore, based on the right to property, the premise that government should redistribute the wealth is false. The government has nothing to give to anybody that it does not first take from somebody else. No government has the right to confiscate the property of one man in order to distribute it to another man. When one comprehends the full meaning of property rights, it is clear that most government programs, such as taxation, inflation, and subsidies, are violations of that right.

To sum up, socialism, by removing the rewards of thinking and action—the profit-motive and property rights—forces its citizens to become slaves to the state. The end result of socialism is progressing impoverishment; products become shabby because there is no pride in workmanship; fewer products from which to choose are available because competition dries up. It is anti-survival, anti-life to work for the common good, to hold no selfish interest, to have no incentive to work. To the individual it means misery and degradation. Only the idle elite are enriched because, as parasites, they profit from the exploitation of the majority who work.

To a society, socialism is sure death. The last great Roman historian, Ammianius Marcellinius, blamed the decline in personal morality and self-determination as the causes of the fall of the Roman Empire.

> . . . the essential cause of Rome's decline lay with her people: their morals . . . their failure to do what was right, their desire to borrow on tomorrow and send the bill to others. . . Economic decay and political decay went hand in hand as they always have and always will. A decentralized social order was replaced by a centralized state-controlled economy and bureaucracy. . . The private citizen abdicated his responsibilities to a central government; and the cost of maintenance crumbled the Roman Nation.[9]

Under laissez-faire capitalism, personal morality and self-determination are a way of life. Business prospers. The peaceful coexistence of sovereign nations is possible. Under socialism it is impossible. Keynesian economics teaches that nationalism is the best internationalism, that hostile policies bring peace, and friendly policies, war, that international currency stability and free trade bring instability and chaos, and that nationalistic and mutually hostile policies bring international stability and prosperity.[10] This is irrational, of course. Socialism fosters trade wars, foreign exchange controls, international hatred, and war. The philosophy of protectionism is a philosophy of war. Life and property are jeopardized. Socialism undermines strong economies; and in the name of law and order, a dictator is elected.

The principles of socialism are self-contradictory. No gov-

---

[9]Brian L. Bex, *The Decline and Fall of the American Republic* (Indiana: The American Communications Network, 1971), pp. 31-32.

[10]Henry Hazlitt, *The Failure of the New Economics* (New York: Van Nostrand Co., 1959), pp. 343-44.

ernment can guarantee freedom and protect private property otherwise than by supporting and defending the free market. The substitution of the welfare state and interventionist policies for the laissez-faire state as practiced for the past four decades by Western governments has resulted in wars, civil wars, ruthless oppression of free people by self-appointed dictators, economic depressions, poverty, mass unemployment, capital consumption, and famines.

The unsurpassed efficiency of capitalism has never before manifested itself in a more profound way than in this age of heinous anti-capitalism. While governments, political parties, and labor unions are sabotaging all business operations, the spirit of free enterprise still succeeds in increasing the quantity and improving the quality of products and in rendering them more easily accessible to the consumers. The majority of people in capitalistic countries enjoy a standard of living today far superior to that of ages gone by.

Nevertheless, capitalism is doomed if the actions which its functioning requires are rejected by a nation's morality, are declared illegal by the laws, and are prosecuted as criminal by the courts. The Roman Empire crumbled to dust because it lacked the spirit of free enterprise and embraced socialism. The policy of interventionism and its political corollary, dictatorship, always disintegrate and destroy free societies.

There is a choice between the free market—capitalism, and bureaucratic whim—socialism. It is within man's power, says Henry Hazlitt, to avert the nightmarish prospect of galloping socialism, to restore order, justice, constitutionalism, limited government, economic and personal liberty, internal peace, and stable prosperity and growth.[11] Man cannot evade deciding between these alternatives by adopting a "middle-of-the road" position. To abolish the free market means complete chaos and the disintegration of the division of labor as it is known today.

The American revolutionary Thomas Paine once said, "These

---

[11]Hazlitt, *Man Vs. The Welfare State*, pp. 215-16.

are the times that try men's souls." No doubt Ammianus Marcellinius had entertained that same thought. Today, men are contemplating the current state of affairs and think that these are the times that try men's souls. All of them are correct. Man's struggle for freedom is eternal. This is why it is imperative to grasp how evil socialism is. Appeasement will not work; compromising will not work. Control is indivisible. Socialism means that one will alone acts; one will alone chooses, decides, directs, acts, and gives orders. The substitution of economic planning for economic freedom removes all freedom and leaves to the individual only the right to obey. There can be no compromise between capitalism and socialism. In any compromise between good and evil, evil always wins. Philosophically they are incompatible and irreconcilable. Practically, the difference between capitalism and socialism is the difference between freedom and slavery.

8

TO THE GLORY OF GOLD

The Founding Fathers were obviously right about their suspicion of government. They tried to insure the usage of gold and silver money so that future generations would not have to fear oppressive taxation and destructive inflation. But the Founding Fathers' great work—the Constitution—was subverted by government when the usage of hard money by American citizens was prohibited.

When gold and silver are outlawed, when man is given no choice, when he is forced to accept paper money for his labor, he is robbed of his reward. He is given scraps of paper instead of real money. The real money he should be receiving for his labor is reserved for governmental use, to be squandered as politicians see fit. In its place the individual is given paper money—paper which is inflated, depreciated, debauched, and debased. He is forced to accept this paper. He is forced because only by force will man part with his property.

The branch of government that is in charge of and interprets the gold laws is the U.S. Treasury Department. According to the Treasury Department, Office of Domestic Gold and Silver Operations' statement of July, 1966, "The basic principles governing the administration of the Gold Acts and Orders are that gold, as a store of value, can be held only by the Government." In other words, the government has appropriated to itself the unconstitutional right to seize its citizens' gold—their protection—and has left a counterfeit pile of paper. Therefore, no one knows how much money he has, how wealthy he is, and how fast his wealth is being embezzled.

The only other major nation, beside the United States and Great Britain, that prohibits the ownership of gold by its citizens is the Soviet Union. Private holdings or transactions in gold are considered there to be "economic crimes"—most serious offenses in a communist-socialist state. Those engaged in them are subject to the firing squad.[1]

The importance of gold ownership is twofold. One, the only true economic barometer is gold. A free price system for commodities and currencies tends to keep the price of gold stable. Inflation forces up prices, including the price of gold. As gold appreciates, paper money depreciates. When the price of gold doubles in relation to the amount of currency in circulation, the value of the currency, or paper dollars, is cut in half. This devaluation of the dollar is the natural outcome of government inflating the money supply, thereby decreasing each unit's worth. Thus, gold measures the extent of inflation.

Money represents the people's wealth. By destroying gold's objective value, an equivalent of wealth produced, the government has the power to confiscate its citizens' property without their knowledge and consent. This is the second reason why gold ownership is important. Once the people lose the intrinsic value of their money, they can expect to lose their freedom as well.

Throughout history, fiat money and tyranny have gone hand in hand. For a recent example, that master of oppression, Adolf Hitler, waged a relentless war on gold to the very end of his brutal and despicable empire. Intrinsic-value money allows the individual to fashion, to a great extent, his own economic destiny; fiat money puts him at the mercy of the state; if the state is sole arbiter of value, then the state can change the value of its money or inflate the supply at will—and the citizen can go whistle for his lost savings. This rather obvious lesson of history was not lost on Hitler, who recognized immediately that gold was an enemy of the authoritarian state and consequently did his best to banish it from the Reich. Fiat money, in the final analysis, can circulate only by fiat, that is, by force, and it inevitably changes

---

[1]Donald J. Hoppe, *How to Invest in Gold Coins* (New York: Arlington House, 1970), p. 58.

any republic into a despotism. People who allow their money to lose its intrinsic value, can expect eventually to lose their freedom as well.[2]

Another master of oppression was Benito Mussolini. He understood the tremendous power that gold carries. Those who control it are in a position to dominate those who do not. As long as the control of gold is in the hands of the people, the people are safe; when the control of gold falls into the hands of government, the people are in trouble. As soon as Mussolini became dictator, he confiscated all the gold and silver. To finance Fascist socialism and to build up his war machine, Mussolini ordered iron kettles to be placed in the streets of Italy. The people, walking by in single file, were forced to toss in the kettles their gold, silver, silverware, and jewelry.

Not only does a tyrannical government need precious metals to finance its wars, but it must also strip the people of their wealth. Should the people accumulate too much wealth, government either outlaws gold possession or floods the country with printing-press money, thereby confiscating the wealth of the people. For this reason, *gold* becomes the *natural enemy* of *socialism*. Sound money and the welfare state cannot exist side by side. One or the other must go.

Since private ownership of gold is essential to the maintenance of freedom, why is the United States government so adamant against the private ownership of gold? If gold were a "barbaric relic," as they claim it is, then why do they prohibit its ownership? It is unnecessary to prohibit the ownership of candles or the horse and buggy. After all, gold is a commodity just like any other commodity. What would happen if the government started prohibiting one commodity after another? If the government considers gold "demonetized," then why all the fuss about its ownership? In our enlightened age of civil rights, if people want to own gold, and who has more right to it than those who earn it, why not let them?

---

[2]*Ibid.*, p. 203.

Is it because if the people were allowed to own gold—gold coins and gold bullion—they would instantly explode the lies they were told, and forced to pretend to believe, about what the paper money is really worth? When government feels obliged to make crimes out of innocent and harmless actions, the government must be trying to cover up something.

Since money is the root of all good and gold is money, then gold, too, must be the root of all good. And an honest hardworking man should be allowed to own and trade gold. It is his right by virtue of the fact that he is supposedly a free man. And a free man must be allowed to own and trade gold in order to remain free.

Speaking of rights, by what right does the government deny the private ownership of gold? If the government does not protect its citizens' rights, who will? And if it does not, then who needs it? After all, the only valid justification of a government is the protection of individual rights. A right that is granted by the favor of those who rule is no longer a right; it becomes a favor that is revocable at will. Since the Constitution specifically calls for gold and silver as legal tender, it would appear that the government has overstepped its authority; it has no right to tamper with the market's choice of a medium of exchange, i.e., the private ownership of gold—an inalienable right.

Using gold as a medium of exchange allows free trade among free men, which is the basis of capitalism. The importance of capitalism is that it develops respect for private property, a high moral fiber within the community (there is no drug or crime problem), a high standard of living, independent men, and freedom and justice for all. Capitalism has created the greatest environment of freedom known to man. It gave the world nearly one hundred years of peace and raised the standard of living to unprecedented heights. The United States, under the gold standard, was known as the "land of opportunity."

Gold, more precisely the gold standard, was the medium of exchange by means of which capitalism brought science and industry into the remotest parts of the world, everywhere destroying age-old prejudices and superstitions, sowing the seeds of life, freeing minds, and creating riches unheard of before. It accompanied the progress of capitalism which united all nations into a community of free nations peacefully cooperating with one another. The gold standard was the world standard of the age of capitalism. It is easy to understand why people viewed the gold standard as the symbol of peace and prosperity throughout the world.

The second half of the book will prove that whenever gold is traded freely, men remain free and economies prosper. Whenever a shortage of gold develops, usually as a result of individual hoarding because of a lack of confidence in government policy, trade slackens and economies stagnate. An acute shortage of gold can lead to a total collapse of civilization, such as the fall of the Roman Empire which precipitated the Dark Ages.

The confidence that gold lends to trade is of prime importance to all men.

In this eternal battle for individual and economic survival, in the name of justice and freedom for all Americans, there is only one weapon with which to fight the onslaught of socialism. This is the weapon that all socialists fear and is the first one they denounce. It is the last bastion of liberty and its final defense. That weapon is the Gold Standard!

PART II

THE GOLD STANDARD

9

THE ANCIENT WORLD GLITTERED WITH GOLD

For thousands of years, from the Orient to Egypt, the ancient world glittered with gold. Above the walls of man's first cities gold shone from temple spires and towers that were raised to the sun.

Gold was the first metal to attract the attention of man because it is one of the few metals that are found in the elemental or free state in nature. Gold nuggets were attractive because only gold exhibited luster; it shone like the sun. It was almost indestructible and immediately useful.

When gold was discovered and man learned that it was so easily shaped, shells, which were valued in ancient times, were reproduced in gold. This gave permanence, strength, and a new beauty to an immemorially old form of ornament.

Metallurgically, gold offered the minimum of problems to early craftsmen. Although heavy, it is extremely soft. It can be cut with a piece of flint and pounded back together again. It can be pulled into wire to be used as pins and fishhooks. Its very permanence gave it a uniquely high position in the early scale of metallic values. As a substance it was very precious because it was very rare. It does not rust, corrode, or tarnish. Copper coins removed from hiding may show a heavy corrosive crust. Silver coins may show stains and tarnish until quite black. But gold coins will gleam as brightly as they did the day they left the mint, two hundred or two thousand years ago.

Gold was regarded as more than a store of worth and as more than a measure of value.

For it has been in a unique degree the decorative metal, loved by the great and wealthy as a means of ostentation, loved by the lesser man (according to his ability to acquire

67

it) because of its beauty of color and sheen and texture in
addition to its intrinsic value, and loved by the goldsmith
because of its splendid working qualities.[1]

Since gold was almost indestructible, it symbolized life, and
thus became the royal metal. Man searched for it, mined it,
stole it, fought over it, and died for it.

Six thousand years ago the Egyptians used four-fifths of the
world's gold to please their 2,000 gods. They used gold for
religious purposes; it was divine. They displayed their wealth
admirably by architecture, sculpture, and painting. These are
evidence of a continuing high taste and of a growing skill for
gold.

The Egyptian rulers had a keen appetite for the precious
metal. At one time Egypt had over one hundred gold mines in
operation. It was the main source of gold used in antiquity.
By royal privilege, the Egyptian rulers jealously guarded and
monopolized the gold mines. Egypt's natural wealth was an
important reason for the power of the successive rulers and of
the continuity of the Egyptian culture.

As the Egyptian civilization advanced, her quest for gold
increased. She intensified her search for gold with a resumption
of foreign conquests. The royal metal became the reason for
war and the prize of battle. To gain gold everything was risked
and anything was fair.

From Egypt onward, civilizations began, grew, and perished
according to their gold supply. Economies absorbed gold or
were injected with it, gaining their wealth by increasing con-
quest or trade, or losing their wealth by sudden subjection. And
all the time the total quantity of gold in existence mounted
steadily and massively.

Persia conquered Egypt. She took over the gold mines and
hoarded the gold. She monopolized and immobilized the world's
gold supply for the greater part of two centuries.

---

[1]C. H. V. Sutherland, *Gold: Its Beauty, Power and Allure* (New York:
McGraw-Hill Co., 1969), p. 19.

Alexander the Great conquered Persia. He seized the royal treasure of Susa and took over its contents: 2,000,000 pounds of gold and silver in the form of ingots and 500,000 pounds of gold coin. Such was the wealth of Persia, which, Greece, a poor nation subsisting on silver, conquered. Gold poured into the world's markets. The center of gold flowed from Asia to Europe, where it remained until the collapse of the Roman Empire.

Around that time pellets of gold and silver alloy were being used as the medium of exchange. But the intrinsic gold-silver proportion of this money could not be easily and accurately assessed. One of the kings of Lydia, Croesus, realized that commerce could be expanded and accelerated by the introduction of an internationally acceptable currency. He introduced a pure gold coin and a pure silver coin, both marked with his royal device of the facing heads of a lion and a bull. In 700 B.C., Croesus originated the world's first true coinage.

The coinage of gold along with the conquests of Alexander the Great released great quantities of gold onto the world's markets. As gold began to circulate, it stimulated trade. Since it was readily available for exchange, substitutes became acceptable. Silver was no longer discriminated against. Merchants were not forced to restrict their trading to the markets where one metal was available or the other acceptable. They were free to roam the world. As they did, commerce expanded and the merchant nations of the West prospered.

The rise of the Roman Empire required vast supplies of gold. Rome's dependence on gold was reflected by the fact that first one gold-producing country after another was annexed until, at its peak, the empire included every source of gold then known to the Western world. Gold enabled Rome's trade to flourish. By buying off foreign mercenaries with gold, Rome protected her borders from foreign invasion.

Under Julius Caesar the denarius was originated. It was a coin of practically pure silver, equivalent to ten pieces of copper. By Nero's time, the alloy in the denarius was ten per cent; under Commodus, thirty per cent, under Septimius, fifty per cent. By A.D. 260 the silver content of the denarius was five per cent. This meant a profit to the Imperial mint, which was issuing unprecedented quantities of cheap coin.

Since the state compelled the acceptance of these debased coins at their face value (legal tender laws) instead of their actual worth, prices rose rapidly. In Egypt inflation ran out of control. A measure of wheat that had cost eight drachmas in the first century cost 120,000 drachmas at the end of the third century. The empire had begun with urbanization and civilization; it was ending in reruralization and barbarism.

Rome started as a Republic with independent, self-reliant citizens. In 27 B.C. she was turned into an Empire by Augustus, who managed to get all the power in his own hands by cheating the people of their freedom. Brian Bex, in his *The Decline and Fall of the American Republic,* likens it to the old "shell game": "The pea of real power was removed from the shell marked 'Republic,' to the one marked 'Empire' so fast and silently that it fooled the onlookers."[2] The historian Gibbon in *The Decline and Fall of the Roman Empire,* explains the technique:

> Augustus was sensible that mankind is governed by names; nor was he deceived in his expectation that the Senate and people would submit to slavery, provided they were respectfully assured that they still enjoyed their ancient freedom.

By A.D. 300 the Empire had decayed to the extent where Diocletian could and did substitute a managed economy for the free market. As dictator he centralized the state, always keeping the constitution preserved in the Senate. He gave food to the poor at no cost to the recipient. He imposed complete state control over industry. The state became a powerful em-ployer, and in some cities, the largest employer. Trade associations and craft guilds received various privileges from the state. He imposed wage and price controls. To support this bureaucracy —the court, the dole, and the public works programs—

---

[2]*Bex*, p. ii.

taxation rose to unprecedented peaks. By the fourth century, flight from taxes became almost epidemic.

By this time the silver and gold mines were drying up. The gold and silver Rome did possess were shipped to China, India, and Africa in payment for the high living of the Roman emperors.

Deeply in debt, the government increased the minting of debauched coinage. The propensity of certain kings and emperors to devalue their coinage by clipping, filing, reducing, or debasing was prolific. The mighty emperors of Imperial Rome were particularly notorious for this dishonesty. In fact, the simplest and oldest variety of monetary inventionism is debasement of coins or diminution of their weight or size for the sake of debt abatement. The Roman authorities assigned to the cheaper currency units the full legal tender power previously granted to the better units.

As inflation and taxation soared, hoarding became commonplace. The people culled out the better coins that came into their hands, hid them, and passed along the degraded or debased coins. The hoarders of gold or silver coins were actually acting in self-defense. It was one way to hedge against continuing inflation, or to put it correctly, the continuing depreciation of money.

The principle was later explained by an English economist named Gresham. Gresham's Law states: bad money drives good money out of circulation (into hiding). This economic law goes into effect whenever governments debase the currency. The ultimate results of the Roman emperors' interference with the free market and the money supply were economic and social disintegration.

The decline of Rome and the decline of its money went hand in hand. Rioting, lawlessness, dishonesty, and corruption were aggravated by the spectacle of emperors and governments that were little more than liars and embezzlers themselves.

From the economic crisis of the third century, largely induced by a corrupt money, the Western Empire never recovered. By the fourth century money had fallen to the degraded position of *ponderata* when it was customary to assay and weigh each piece offered in payment. And by the seventh century, the weights themselves had been so frequently degraded that it was no longer possible to make a specific bargain for money. There was no law to define the weight of a pound or an ounce and no power to enforce the law if one existed. Under these circumstances money became extinct. Nor, we are reminded, was it the only institution that perished; all institutions perished. There was no government except the sword, there was no law, there were no certain weights and measures, exchanges were made in kind, or for slaves, or bags of corn, or lumps of metal, which men weighed or counted to one another holding the thing to be sold in one hand, the thing bought in the other.

No more fittingly can we close this comment on the failure of the Romans to cope with money than by quoting the words of one Antonius Augustus, cited by Del Mar, "Money had more to do with the distemper of the Roman Empire than the Huns or the Vandals."[3]

Upon Rome's collapse the barbarians who invaded Europe continued gold coinage of good quality. Although this released much gold currency, which, until then, had been hoarded away out of fear and lack of confidence, gold coin minting, which had continued between A.D. 500-700 in France and Spain and briefly in Britain, ceased. By 700 there was not enough gold available to guarantee an economy based on gold coins. The gold supply had finally reached a point of scarcity where a gold currency was impossible. Coins in France were debased from gold to silver. This acute lack of gold in Europe existed for five centuries, from 700-1200.

At the moment of the collapse of the Roman Empire in the West, gold had been used for over 4,000 years to balance econo-

---

[3]Elgin Groseclose, *Money, Man and Morals* (New York: Christian Freedom Foundation, Inc., 1963), p. 8.

mies and to measure and store wealth. It changed form, of course, but it never perished. With the decline of one power and the rise of another it was always on the move. The gold which first belonged to Egypt, then Persia, then Greece, and later Rome, now flowed to the Byzantine Empire in the east, which unshaken by the collapse of the Roman half of the world, had embarked on a period of commercial prosperity.

The monetary lesson of Rome was well learned by Constantine, the founder of the Byzantine Empire. He knew that confidence in its honesty and integrity is the strongest type of power a government can possess. Under Greek influence he established a new monetary system based on the gold coin—the *bezant*.

The bezant was minted at a standard of 65 grains of fine gold for *800 years*—undoubtedly the most outstanding achievement in the history of money. So determined were the empire's rulers to maintain the integrity of their money that they required all bankers and others through whose hands money passed to take an oath never to file, clip or debase coins in any manner. The penalty for any violation of this oath: the offender's hand was cut off.

The Byzantine Empire survived for over 1,200 years, until A.D. 1453. Its people prospered; its culture flourished. No enemy dared attack its capital. The bezant was the standard of value throughout the world. In fact, one of the most interesting lessons that can be learned from the Byzantine monetary experience is that despite the constant and free export of bezants to all parts of the medieval world, there was never any "shortage" of gold.

The stability of Byzantium attracted all the world's gold. The immense wealth that was amassed is almost incomprehensible by today's standards: Emperor Anastasius at his death in A.D. 518 left a personal treasure of 320,000 pounds of gold. Theodora in 856 handed over 109,000 pounds of gold, and Basil II in the tenth century possessed 200,000 pounds of gold. Add to this the wealth in private holdings of 2,000 to 3,000 pounds of gold plus great stocks of gold held as church treasure and it is clear how the total wealth of the Byzantine Empire caused a gold famine that spread over Western Europe after A.D. 700.

During the Dark Ages, from 500-1500, gold virtually disappeared from currency; it was restricted for the adornment of kings. The Dark Ages was a period of monetary debauchery throughout medieval Europe. In the eleventh century Byzantine currency debasement started. The gold then flowed back to Europe through trade with the Arabs and the crusaders. But the transition over the major part of Europe from acute poverty to relative prosperity was a long and difficult process. By 1400, however, economies were expanding again. Gold was in great demand. Gold coinage started between 1324 and 1325. By 1500, Europe was again stocked with good supplies of gold.

Gold gave new life to commerce. Gold and silver were the values placed on new lands. Portugal received gold from Africa and Japan. Spain discovered vast supplies of gold in Mexico and South America. In the 107 years from Columbus' landing, the total gold brought back to Spain was 750,000 pounds. Emperor Charles of Spain monopolized the gold supply of Europe. He knew that the joint prosperity of Spain and Europe depended on the prompt arrival of the treasure fleets.

Banking centers in Lisbon, Seville, Antwerp, Vienna and Genoa acquired great wealth by financing the trade which they stimulated. Any European nation of consequence, by then, had to present a gold currency that was not only handsome but profuse. The gold coins of Europe continued to increase in size. Henry IV of Spain issued a gold piece weighing half a pound!

The multiplication of gold supplies in the fifteenth and sixteenth centuries led to a position whereby control of the price and movement of the metal began to slip from the grasp of kings into the hands of merchant bankers and goldsmiths in the larger centers of commerce.

The people entrusted the goldsmiths with their gold rather than an agency of the Crown. By leaving gold with goldsmiths in markets wherever they traveled, merchants found that a receipt signed by a known and trusted goldsmith of the community was as readily negotiable as gold itself. The receipts became the first bank notes—payable to the bearer on demand. They were supplemented by bills of exchange which instructed the goldsmith to transfer a part of the depositor's gold to the man who presented the signed note. The paper was lighter to carry, safer from theft, and could always be exchanged for gold when desired.

The smiths then discovered they had more than enough gold on hand to cover all the receipts presented for payment at any one time. So they loaned out some of the gold at interest. In so doing the goldsmiths became the world's first bankers and the first to establish a system of credit. In addition, they gained control of the gold bullion market, which has continued to this day.

Following the Dark Ages was an age in which great volumes of gold and silver were discovered. Since production still lagged behind the influx of gold, prices rose. But the Industrial Revolution in eighteenth century England began a process by which Europe severed its bondage from the lever, the pulley, and the screw, and productivity swiftly regained a relationship with the growth in gold supplies. England became one of the foremost gold markets of the world.

In the meantime, gold had recovered its position long traditional in ancient civilizations, from which it had been dislodged by the disorder and running down of medieval economies. It had again become the universally prized metal and universally desired as a measure of value and as a store of wealth.

10

THE CALIFORNIA GOLD RUSH

The vast gold supplies that had been found in Mexico, South America, Japan and Africa wiped out the deep poverty of the Dark Ages and lifted Europe into the era of the Industrial Revolution. Those discoveries were merely a prelude to the next El Dorado—the California gold rush of 1849, which is one of the most fascinating episodes in the history of gold.

Innumerable finds of gold of immense richness had been made throughout the history of gold, which spans 6,000 years. But none could compare or even match the California boom of 1849. It held limitless attraction to men from every part of the world; its vast wealth catapulted the United States into a world leader; the industrial developments brought forth from the mines launched the era of the American Industrial Revolution. And the romantic tales of the Old West are a favorite subject to Americans of all ages.

The California gold rush was a new phenomenon, unparalleled in man's history with the precious metal. For the first time in history the gold belonged exclusively to the man who discovered it. The United States of America was a free country; California was a free territory; and the gold in this big country was free for the finding. It was the property of the man who found it; it was his property to do with as he pleased. There were no gods, kings, landowners, or governments demanding a share (and what government agents did exist were very ineffective). It was every man for himself and by 1849 there were 100,000 of them. Considered as a whole, the mass migration to California was on a truly colossal scale. Men came from the four corners of the globe, spoke a dozen different languages, and represented every walk of life. Some came halfway around the world around Cape Horn, arriving at San Francisco in vessels that were, by then, only fit to rot![1]

The ambition of the California forty-niner was the fuel that started and propelled the California gold rush. He was a rugged individual, whose highest value was life. He loved life and he loved the thought of striking it rich. For that goal he endured incredible hardships. His life consisted of hard physical labor, insufficient shelter of brush or canvas, and a diet that was monotonous and inadequate. He suffered from scurvy, dysentery, and typhoid.[2]

Food shortages, insufficient shelter, and diseases were a common threat to the forty-niner's life. It took an industrial revolution to improve them. But the protection of life and property, which was under his direct control, was effectively protected. The forty-niners formed an informal kind of government where no government or court system had existed. As a strike was made, they gathered together and agreed on the laws for each new district. These laws regulated the size and number of claims each man could stake and the way they should be marked. They agreed on the actions to be considered crimes and the appropriate punishment.

On Sunday when most of the prospectors were in camp, they held town meetings. The majority ruled and the decision was final. Since there were no jails, crimes were punished immediately. The most immoral crime was theft. A man who was accused of stealing tools or provisions from another man's claim could be tried, convicted, and hanged within an hour. If it were a lesser crime, the culprit might be banished from the district; or he was branded, so that his criminal record was known to all who later met him.

It was a harsh sort of justice, but it was swift. The laws that were established were enforced. Law and order prevailed. Life and property were protected. A gold-rush chronicler, Bayard Taylor, reported, "The capacity of the people for self-government was never so triumphantly illustrated."

---

[1]Sutherland, *Gold: Its Beauty, Power and Allure*, p. 156.
[2]Gina Allen, *Gold!* (New York: Thomas Y. Crowell Co., 1964), p. 166.

Were the forty-niners really fair? Most emphatically, yes! Into the national code of mining regulations that the government drew up in 1865 were incorporated the forty-niners' principles and provisions that pertained to mining and mineral rights. The national code of mining regulations of 1865 still governs the mining industry today throughout the United States.

The California gold rush represented private enterprise functioning at its best. Although state funds were available, they were abandoned in favor of a system whereby privately mined gold could be bought by the state if it wanted to buy it. Never before had individual enterprise been applied on such a vast scale. It was the century of individual freedom and enterprise. It was the age of the individual.

Although the miners' equipment consisted mostly of picks, pans, and shovels, the yield between 1851 and 1855 was running at a rate of *175,000 pounds* of gold a year, with a peak around *200,000* in 1853. (At that time gold was selling between $12 and $16 an ounce.)

The forty-niner's reward was just and immediate—value for value. Since he was free to produce, to trade, and to profit, profit he did: at Carson Hill, a nugget was discovered that weighed 195 pounds and was valued at $74,000. (A replica of the Carson Hill nugget can be seen at Knott's Berry Farm, Buena Park, California.) North of Carson Hill at Angel's Camp, a prospector named Raspberry dug $7,000 worth of ore in three days, opening the mine that eventually made him a millionaire.

Between 1851 and 1855, California produced what it had taken ancient Rome half a century to win from northwestern Spain. In the ten years after the discovery at Sutter's Mill, California produced $555 million in gold. And it is said that there is more gold still in California than has ever been taken out!

For a quarter of a century forty-niners blazed trails across the frontier, opening up the West. As towns that followed the gold discoveries grew, civilization developed. In 1850, California gained statehood.

The forty-niners produced the gold that financed industry and commerce. Many industrial techniques were invented and developed in the mine, such as mass production, the 24-hour day, and the division of labor. Brought from the mine, they changed craftsmen's shops into factories. Machines were copied topside to speed the production and distribution of the world's goods. From the mine came the steam engine, the railway, the subway, the elevator, the escalator, artificial light and artificial air.[3] The knowledge that was obtained from the California gold rush led to gold discoveries in Australia in 1851, in the Comstock Lode in Nevada in 1859, in South Africa in 1866, and in Alaska in 1897.

The ambition and courage of the California forty-niner not only benefited the industrious miner, but was of immense benefit to the United States. Following the gold rush era, the United States was to become the most productive and wealthiest country in history. In recognition of the California forty-niners' achievements, the railroad track that first linked the East Coast with the West was joined, in 1869, at Promontory Point, Utah, with a golden spike.[4]

The California gold rush stimulated a worldwide search for gold. It launched the gold exploitation era. Henceforth, gold was more diligently sought in all parts of the world, and when found was immediately exploited.

The first gold discovery was in Australia. The loss of people as a result of the magnitude of the emigration to California from Australia was worrying Australian officials. So in 1851 they formed the Gold Discovery Committee. The Committee offered a reward of 200 pounds to anyone who discovered gold within 200 miles of Melbourne. Within one year it was claimed. Within the next ten years 1,750,000 pounds of gold were produced in Victoria. The discovery of one nugget in 1869 was appropriately named the Welcome Stranger. It weighed nearly 160 pounds.

In 1859, the Comstock Lode in Nevada only four miles long and lasting twenty years was the second discovery. It

---

[3]*Ibid.*, p. 155-56.
[4]*Ibid.*, p. 184.

produced America's primary source of gold. Gold was also discovered in Colorado, Montana, and South Dakota, where old Homestake mine remains to this day the only sizable producer of gold in the United States.

In 1866, gold was discovered in South Africa in the world-famous Main Reef Group. Today it takes an investment of $50 to $100 million to dig the first ounce of gold from a South African mine, hardly the kind of cash a prospector carried around in his poke. The gold belonged not to a poor man with a pick, but to the investor with capital. The South African mines produce over a billion dollars worth of gold a year, almost eighty per cent of the output of the non-communist world.

The day of the poor man's mining was not quite over. One more rich goldfield remained to be discovered, in which every man was free to dig for himself, to get rich, or in this case, to freeze. The fourth El Dorado was in Alaska. In 1897, Dawson City sprung up in the Klondike area of the Yukon River in Alaska, as near to the North Pole as northern Siberia.

Here cold was the enemy. A prospector's thermometer was unable to tell him how cold it was because at forty-two degrees below zero the mercury froze; kerosene refused to pour at fifty-five degrees; at seventy-two degrees below the pain-killer turned solid. If the Hudson's Bay rum froze, it was eighty degrees below and no one ventured outside.

Despite the cold, scurvy, and gangrenous limbs, the search for gold continued. Those who survived the winter to bring back their prize, stepped off the ships with missing and mutilated toes, fingers, ears, and noses, caused by the bitter cold of the north. But they carried gold.

Within two years, Dawson City produced $32 million worth of gold.

From 1850 to 1900, the estimated gold produced from these five major goldfields was 23,000,000 pounds or *twenty per cent of all the gold ever produced in the world to date.*

11

THE DOMESTIC GOLD STANDARD

Although gold was available during the American Revolution, the Continental Congress used fiat money as an expediency.

In the aftermath, the Founding Fathers supported the gold standard. They did not support it passively or theoretically; they supported it in knockdown, drag-out fights in the political arena (including one rebellion). Jefferson and Madison, in particular, were hard-money men and campaigned vigorously for gold and against paper money.

They had learned their lesson the hard way and learned it well. The four words "not worth a Continental" recall the runaway inflation that very nearly destroyed the American Revolution.

"Continentals" were the paper money issued by the second Continental Congress to finance the Revolutionary War. It began in June, 1775, when the Continental Congress voted the first and supposedly last issue of $2,000,000 of paper "bills of credit," to be redeemed in silver after 1779. It ended in 1781 when the issuance of state and Continental paper totaled $240,000,000 and $210,000,000 respectively. As in every inflation, the notes were at first issued in moderate amounts and small denominations. But as depreciation set in, larger and larger issues were made, at shorter and shorter intervals.

During those terrifying years commodity prices soared. In 1777, a Bostonian wrote, "We are all starving here, since this plague addition to the regulating bill. People will not bring in provision, and we cannot procure the necessities of life." In the "mild" winter that followed, the army at Valley Forge suffered agonies for want of food, clothing, and blankets that simply could not be purchased in the controlled market. At the same time Americans were selling food and goods to the British in nearby

Cont.

Philadelphia for hard money. By 1778, prices were up 480 per cent from prewar levels.

Inflation was out of control. As each paper issue added to the glut of dollars in private hands, Congress had to make the next issue substantially larger to pay for the same amount of supplies. The states were forced to make Continentals legal tender. That is, sellers were forced to accept the notes at face value or forfeit their goods in penalty. Price controls and ceilings were adopted, enforceable by stiff fines and imprisonment. These laws did more to keep goods off the market than to keep notes circulating.

Congress went so far as to declare ". . . that any person who shall hereafter be so lost to all virtue and regard for his country as to refuse to receive said bills in payment, or obstruct and discourage the currency or circulation thereof . . . shall be deemed . . . an enemy of his country."

But it was no use. The people would not accept worthless paper in exchange for their valuable goods, even on penalty of death. By 1781, it took one thousand Continentals to buy one dollar in specie (hard money).

The Continental inflation caused immense losses and unquestionably prolonged the war by several years. It had so badly damaged the nation's ability to carry on the war that only loans from France in the latter years saved the Revolution. Robert Morris, a financial genius, was able to use the loans (mostly in the form of supplies, but some gold) to put the war effort on a hard-money basis at the end, and thus helped gain the victory so long delayed by financial distress. Only when the inflation had run its full inevitable course did gold and silver coin "come out of hiding" (as it always does after an inflation) to start the exhausted nation toward recovery.

The havoc of paper money during the war had ruined the country's economy. After the war the economy suffered from deflation. The general complaint about the state of private and public finance was that hard money was scarce and growing scarcer, and paper money (resorted to again in the 1780s in seven states) was a threat and growing more threatening. The critical problem was the alarming shortage of specie. The drain of specie kept the back country in a state of political and social tension. The balance of trade was so drastically against the United States that even the most solid merchants wondered how long their credit would hold up in Europe.

To put an end to paper money, the Articles of Confederation, the first constitution of the original thirteen states, in 1781, prohibited the issuance of bills of credit by the national government. When the second and final constitution was adopted in 1787, the hard-money issue was still very much alive. For "what John Jay derided as 'the doctrine of the political transubstantiation of paper into gold and silver' had a powerful appeal to men with crushing debts and unpopular taxes to pay and with no coin in which to pay them."[1]

James Madison came to the aid of the hard-money people. He defended the value of gold and silver money over paper money. On January 25, 1788, he wrote the forty-fourth letter of the Federalist Papers in which he eloquently and effectively summed up the justice that only hard money can produce:

> The extension of the prohibition to bills of credit must give pleasure to every citizen in proportion to his love of justice and his knowledge of the true springs of public prosperity. The loss which America has sustained since the peace, from the pestilent effects of paper money on the necessary confidence between man and man, on the necessary confidence in the public councils, on the industry and morals of the people, and on the character of republican government, constitutes an enormous debt against the States chargeable with this unadvised measure, which must long remain unsatisfied; or rather an accumulation of guilt, which can be expiated no otherwise than by a voluntary sacrifice on the altar of justice, of the power which has been the instrument of it . . . the States . . . ought not to be at liberty to substitute a paper medium in the place of coin. . . The power to make anything but gold and silver a tender in payment of debts, is

---

[1] Clinton Rossiter, *1787 The Grand Convention*, p. 44.

withdrawn from the States on the same principle with that of issuing a paper currency.[2]

The hard-money people were victorious. As a result of their persistent effort, Article I, Section 10, of the United States Constitution says: "No state shall . . . make anything but gold and silver coin a tender in payment of debts."

The honesty and integrity of men such as Thomas Jefferson, an extremely hard money man whose economic philosophy advocated a one hundred per cent gold standard, produced justice in the marketplace. Jefferson, in particular, knew that gold was the money of the honest productive man. Gold protected the working man from inflation; it enabled him to receive his wages or profits in currency of full value; it enabled him to save without having the value of his savings depreciate. Jefferson knew that paper money oppresses the poor and those on fixed incomes. It was paper that robbed the poor to give to the rich. Only paper created an unearned transfer of wealth from the working and middle classes to the debtor element and those who created the paper money—central banks and governments. With paper money, the rich grow richer and the poor grow poorer. Only the gold standard can insure economic justice; it makes these unearned transfers of wealth impossible. It thus protects the rights of the working and middle classes—the backbone of the nation.

Although the hard-money issue was victorious over paper money, there was one more battle that remained to be won—defeat of the United States central bank. Jefferson, as a skillful politician, welded the pro-gold interests into a powerful political movement (which remains today and forms the basis for modern-day populism) against the paper money forces as represented by Hamilton and the proponents of the Bank of the United States. This battle raged for a generation and culminated in 1832 with Andrew Jackson and the triumph of the pro-gold forces.

With gold and silver as lawful money and the central bank of the United States abolished, the United States was officially on the gold standard.

---

[2]Alexander Hamilton, John Jay, James Madison, *The Federalist* (New York: Random House, The Modern Library, n.d.), pp. 290-91.

12

THE INTERNATIONAL GOLD STANDARD

The magnitude of the gold discoveries in the late eighteen hundreds made available to the world vast supplies of gold. This enabled most nations to adopt gold as their medium of exchange. By 1900, nearly all developed nations respected gold as money and trusted the gold standard as the only objective and effective method to secure the worth of their national currencies and their national prosperity.

At the turn of the century practically every economist of integrity supported the gold standard. The reason was simple: when a nation inflated its money supply, prices rose, gold flowed out of the country, the gold supply was reduced, prices came down, inflation was under control, gold flowed back into the country, prices leveled off. Only the gold standard could protect the individual's wealth and the nation's prosperity from inflation.

The gold standard requires neither rules nor regulations, no legislation or government control, merely the individual freedom to own gold. Of course this freedom of gold ownership embodies the freedom not only to buy and sell for use in industrial production, but also to employ it in exchange, as money. The gold standard is a monetary system in which *gold is proper money* and all paper money is merely a substitute that is payable in gold. This means that in addition to the right to own gold and to use it for money, any paper money issued must be backed one hundred per cent by gold bullion or gold coins and is fully redeemable into gold. Under the gold standard the United States dollar is a piece of gold of a certain weight and fineness. The legal tender is gold. Money is gold and gold is money. Monetary freedom means the gold standard.

Monetary freedom in the United States was short-lived, however. The early history of the American currency clearly illustrates the danger of government interference in the free market's choice of a medium of exchange. Instead of leaving to the free market the function of determining the size, weight, and value of money, it was considered proper for government to regulate the money supply. And since governments were generally biased in favor of the largest possible money supply, which was thought to generate national wealth and prosperity, they favored a double standard in which gold and silver were legal money. But instead of letting both metals circulate side by side at ratios that were freely determined in the money market in accordance with supply and demand, governments felt called upon to regulate their mutual exchange ratios. This regulation was, of course, price fixing of the metals in terms of each other. The inevitable failure of the regulated bimetallic standard due to the operation of Gresham's Law led to either the gold standard or the silver standard; and the fixed ratio between the two determined the outcome.

The first coinage ratio of gold and silver that Alexander Hamilton, Secretary of the Treasury, chose was fixed at 15 to 1. But this ratio overvalued silver and thus drove gold coins out of circulation. When Congress became aware of the disequilibrium in the specie currency, it endeavored to bring the country back to the bimetallic basis. Hence, Congress passed an act on June 23, 1834 which reduced the gold content of the dollar from 24.75 grains pure gold to 23.2 grains, but left the bullion content of the silver dollar unchanged. The reduction of the bullion content of the gold dollar changed the coinage ratio from 15 to 1 to approximately 16 to 1. But just as the earlier ratio had overvalued silver, the new ratio overvalued gold. Consequently, in time, gold began to replace silver as the standard money. Silver coins and silver bullion disappeared from circulation in the same way that they have disappeared from circulation today. The only difference being that today overvalued copper-nickel coins have driven silver into hiding, whereas early Americans drove silver into hiding by spending overvalued gold coins.

What had actually happened was that the Constitution had created a bimetallic system by making gold and silver tender in payment of debts. Then instead of leaving well enough alone, the government interfered with the gold/silver ratio and thereby forced first gold and then silver out of circulation. By so doing, the banks had no choice but to substitute gold reserves for silver specie and a single standard emerged—the gold standard.

The gold standard was honored until 1862, when Congress suspended specie payments because of the Civil War. In place of hard money, Congress enacted a legal tender law, which forced people to accept paper money, and the country entered the greenback era.

Although greenbacks were the only legal money in the Union during and after the Civil War, there was monetary freedom in California. And Calfornians preferred gold. They continued to use gold as their money. Business transactions were conducted in gold, and money substitutes, such as bank notes and deposits, were payable in gold. Since the people were free to choose between paper money and gold currency, they naturally chose gold. And this choice then forced all issuers of paper money also to make payments in gold lest their paper fall in utter disrepute and cease to function as money.

By an Act of Congress on January 14, 1875, specie payments were to be resumed on January 1, 1879. It took four years to coin enough gold to return to hard-money convertibility. Knowing that the government was minting gold at a prodigious rate to meet all demands, the people again trusted the government's integrity and ability to meet its published commitments. The confidence of the people had been restored by the government's actions to fulfill its earlier promise of redemption. There was no crisis, no bank "run" and, as a result, the premium on gold disappeared at once. The gold standard was not officially resumed until Congress passed the Gold Standard Act on March 14, 1900, when the dollar became the "standard unit of value," of twenty-five and four-fifths grains of ninety per cent fine gold.

By that time several European nations had adopted the gold standard. This evolved from the abundance of newly mined gold and the leader in world trade and finance, Great Britain, having adopted the gold standard nearly fifty years earlier. It is interesting to note that Great Britain ended up on the gold standard in much the same way as did the United States. By interfering in the money markets the British government unknowingly changed the "pound sterling" into the "pound gold."

France in 1867 made it clear that only gold could provide the basis for a workable system of interlocking national currencies. Germany went over to gold after the Franco-Prussian War, Austria-Hungary after 1892, and Russia from 1897. They achieved a transition from other standards, silver or irredeemable fiat, through substitution. Silver or paper money were exchanged for gold through the operations of their central banks.

It is significant that it was not monetary freedom that gave birth to the nineteenth-century gold standards. There was no laissez-faire in monetary matters during this century of individual freedom and enterprise.

> The demonetization of silver and the establishment of gold monometallism was the outcome of deliberate government interference with monetary matters . . . it must not be forgotten that it was not the intention of the governments to establish the gold standard. What the governments aimed at was the double standard. They wanted to substitute a rigid, government-decreed exchange ratio between gold and silver for the fluctuating market ratios between the independently coexistent gold and silver coins. The monetary doctrines underlying these endeavors misconstrued the market phenomena in that complete way in which only bureaucrats can misconstrue them. The attempts to create a double standard of both metals, gold and silver, failed lamentably. It was this failure which generated the gold standard. The emergence of the gold standard was the manifestation of a crushing defeat of the governments and their cherished doctrines.[1]

By 1900, most of the leading countries of the world were on the gold standard. The international gold standard had evolved without intergovernmental treaties and institutions. No one had to make the gold standard work as an international

---

[1]Mises, *Human Action*, p. 471.

system. When the leading nations had adopted gold as their currency the world had an international money.

The gold standard united the world as international payments ceased to be a problem. It facilitated world trade and finance, and thereby promoted a worldwide division of labor. The gold standard encouraged exportation of capital from the industrial countries to the backward areas, and thus improved the living conditions of millions of people.[2] It is easy to understand why people viewed the gold standard as the symbol of capitalism— of peace and prosperity.

It is also easy to understand why every economist, at the turn of the century, supported the gold standard. For nearly one hundred years there had existed the longest peace and the greatest prosperity in modern history as a direct result of the capitalistic system, whose medium of exchange was the gold standard.

---

[2]Hans Sennholz, *Inflation or Gold Standard?* (Lansing, Michigan: Constitutional Alliance, Inc., n.d.), pp. 6-7.

13

ECONOMIC FREEDOM AND GOLD

The gold standard presupposes individual freedom, private property, and free markets. It allows freedom to all. Every man is the master of his own future.

Socialists seem to understand—perhaps more clearly and subtly than many defenders of laissez-faire capitalism—that economic freedom and gold are inseparable, that the gold standard is an instrument of capitalism and that each implies and requires the other. This explains why socialists of all persuasions unite in an almost hysterical antagonism toward the gold standard.

In order to understand why the gold standard is an integral part of capitalism—of economic freedom—and why it is the source of socialist antagonism, it is necessary to understand the specific role of gold as a store of value in a free society.

Alan Greenspan, President of Townsend-Greenspan & Co., Inc., economic consultants, has written an excellent article, entitled "Gold and Economic Freedom." The following paragraphs are excerpts from his article, which explains the crucial role of gold in a free society.

The existence of such a commodity [e.g., gold], is a precondition of a division of labor economy. If men did not have some commodity of objective value which was generally acceptable as money, they would have to resort to primitive barter or be forced to live on self-sufficient farms and forgo the inestimable advantages of specialization. If men had no means to store value, i.e., to save, neither long-range planning nor exchange would be possible. . . .

[However,] if all goods and services were to be paid for in gold, large payments would be difficult to execute, and this would tend to limit the extent of a society's division of labor and specialization. Thus a logical extension of the creation of a medium of exchange, is the development of a banking system and credit instruments (bank notes and deposits) which act as a substitute for, but are convertible into, gold.

A free banking system based on gold is able to extend credit and thus to create bank notes (currency) and deposits, according to the production requirements of the economy. Individual owners of gold are induced, by payments of interest, to deposit their gold in a bank (against which they can draw checks). But since it is rarely the case that all depositors want to withdraw all their gold at the same time, the banker need keep only a fraction of his total deposits in gold as reserves. This enables the banker to loan out more than the amount of his gold deposits (which means that he holds claims to gold rather than gold as security for his deposits). But the amount of loans which he can afford to make is not arbitrary: he has to gauge it in relation to his reserves and to the status of his investments.

When banks loan money to finance productive and profitable endeavors, the loans are paid off rapidly and bank credit continues to be generally available. But when the business ventures financed by bank credit are less profitable and slow to pay off, bankers soon find that their loans outstanding are excessive relative to their gold reserves, and they begin to curtail new lending, usually by charging higher interest rates. This tends to restrict the financing of new ventures and requires the existing borrowers to improve their profitability before they can obtain credit for further expansion. Thus, under the gold standard, a free banking system stands as the protector of an economy's stability and balanced growth.

When gold is accepted as the medium of exchange by most, or all nations, an unhampered free international gold standard serves to foster a world-wide division of labor and the broadest international trade. Even though the units of exchange (the dollar, the pound, the franc, etc.) differ from country to country, when all are defined in terms of gold the economies of the different countries act as one—so long as there are no restraints on trade or on the movement of capital. Credit, interest rates, and prices tend to follow similar patterns in all countries. For example, if banks in one country extend credit too liberally, interest rates in that country will tend to fall, inducing depositors to shift their gold to higher-interest paying banks in other countries. This will immediately cause a shortage of bank reserves in the "easy money" country, inducing tighter credit standards and a return to competitively higher interest rates again.

A fully free banking system and fully consistent gold standard have not as yet been achieved. But prior to World War I, the banking system in the United States (and in most of the world) was based on gold, and even though governments intervened occasionally, banking was more free than controlled. Periodically, as a result of overly rapid credit expansion, banks became loaned up to the limit of their gold reserves, interest rates rose sharply, new credit was cut off, and the economy went into a sharp, but short-lived recession. (Compared with the depressions of 1920 and 1932, the pre-World War I business declines were mild indeed.) It was limited gold reserves that stopped the unbalanced expansions of business activity, before they could develop into the post-World War I type of disaster. The readjustment periods were short and the economies quickly re-established a sound basis to resume expansion.

But the process of cure was misdiagnosed as the disease: if shortage of bank reserves was causing a business decline— argued economic interventionists—why not find a way of supplying increased reserves to the banks so they never need be short! If banks can continue to loan money indefinitely— it was claimed—there need never be any slumps in business. And so the Federal Reserve System was organized in 1913. It consisted of twelve regional Federal Reserve banks nominally owned by private bankers, but in fact government sponsored, controlled, and supported. Credit extended by these banks is in practice (though not legally) backed by the taxing power of the federal government. Technically, we remained on the gold standard; individuals were still free to own gold, and gold continued to be used as bank reserves. But now, in addition to gold, credit extended by the Federal Reserve banks ("paper" reserves) could serve as legal tender to pay depositors.

When business in the United States underwent a mild contraction in 1927, the Federal Reserve created more paper reserves in the hope of forestalling any possible bank reserve shortage. More disastrous, however, was the Federal Reserve's attempt to assist Great Britain who had been losing gold to us because the Bank of England refused to allow interest rates to rise when market forces dictated (it was politically unpalatable). The reasoning of the authorities involved was as follows: if the Federal Reserve pumped excessive paper reserves into American banks, interest rates in the United States would fall to a level comparable with those in Great Britain; this would act to stop Britain's gold loss and avoid the political embarrassment of having to raise interest rates.

The "Fed" succeeded: it stopped the gold loss, but it nearly destroyed the economies of the world, in the process. The excess credit which the Fed pump into the economy spilled over into the stock market—triggering a fantastic speculative boom. Belatedly, Federal Reserve officials attempted to sop up the excess reserves and finally succeeded in braking the boom. But it was too late: by 1929 the speculative imbalances had become so overwhelming that the attempt precipitated a sharp retrenching and a consequent demoralizing of business confidence. As a result, the American economy collapsed. Great Britain fared even worse, and rather than absorb the full consequences of her previous folly, she abandoned the gold standard completely in 1931, tearing asunder what remained of the fabric of confidence and inducing a world-wide series of bank failures. The world economies plunged into the Great Depression of the 1930's.

With a logic reminiscent of a generation earlier, statists

argued that the gold standard was largely to blame for the credit debacle which led to the Great Depression. If the gold standard had not existed, they argued, Britain's abandonment of gold payments in 1931 would not have caused the failure of banks all over the world. (The irony was that since 1913, we had been, not on a gold standard, but on what may be termed "a *mixed* gold standard"; yet it is gold that took the blame.)

But the opposition to the gold standard in any form—from a growing number of welfare-state advocates—was prompted by a much subtler insight: the realization that the gold standard is incompatible with chronic deficit spending (the hallmark of the welfare state). Stripped of its academic jargon, the welfare state is nothing more than a mechanism by which governments confiscate the wealth of the productive members of a society to support a wide variety of welfare schemes. A substantial part of the confiscation is effected by taxation. But the welfare statists were quick to recognize that if they wished to retain political power, the amount of taxation had to be limited and they had to resort to programs of massive deficit spending, i.e., they had to borrow money, by issuing government bonds, to finance welfare expenditures on a large scale.

Under a gold standard, the amount of credit that an economy can support is determined by the economy's tangible assets, since every credit instrument is ultimately a claim on some tangible asset. But government bonds are not backed by tangible wealth, only by the government's promise to pay out of future tax revenues, and cannot easily be absorbed by the financial markets. A large volume of new government bonds can be sold to the public only at progressively higher interest rates. Thus, government deficit spending under a gold standard is severely limited.

The abandonment of the gold standard made it possible for the welfare statists *to use the banking system* as a means to an unlimited expansion of credit. They have created paper reserves in the form of government bonds which—through a complex series of steps—the banks accept in place of tangible assets and treat as if they were an actual deposit, i.e., as the equivalent of what was formerly a deposit of gold. The holder of a government bond or of a bank deposit created by paper reserves believes that he has a valid claim on a real asset. But the fact is that there are now more claims outstanding than real assets.

The law of supply and demand is not to be conned. As the supply of money (of claims) increases relative to the supply of tangible assets in the economy, prices must eventually rise. Thus the earnings saved by the productive members of the society lose value in terms of goods. When the economy's books are finally balanced, one finds that this loss in value represents the goods purchased by the government for welfare or other purposes with the money proceeds of the government bonds financed by bank credit expansion.

In the absence of the gold standard, there is no way to protect savings from confiscation through inflation. There is no safe store of value. If there were, the government would have to make its holding illegal, as was done in the case of gold. If everyone decided, for example, to convert all his bank deposits to silver or copper or any other good, and thereafter declined to accept checks as payment for goods, bank deposits would lose their purchasing power and government-created bank credit would be worthless as a claim on goods. The financial policy of the welfare state requires that there be no way for the owners of wealth to protect themselves.

This is the shabby secret of the welfare statists' tirades against gold. Deficit spending is simply a scheme for the "hidden" confiscation of wealth. Gold stands in the way of this insidious process. It stands as a protector of property rights. If one grasps this, one has no difficulty in understanding the statists' antagonism toward the gold standard.[1]

---

[1]Alan Greenspan, "Gold and Economic Freedom," *Capitalism: The Unknown Ideal* (New York: The New American Library, 1962). © Copyright 1966 by The Objectivist, Inc., pp. 89, 91-95. Reprinted by permission.

Since political freedom requires economic freedom and gold and economic freedom are inseparable, it becomes clear why the gold standard has been a point of contention between free enterprisers and socialists.

The gold standard is a monetary system that is basically a regulating device, a feedback mechanism which acts as a regulator to maintain a certain balance. The more play allowed in such a mechanism, the more the balance is jeopardized. Thus, after World War I, the brake exerted by the gold standard had been, if not removed, at least considerably loosened. Once play was allowed, it became possible to surrender to the great tide of prosperity and inflation. But the day the snag occurred, it was necessary to go as far down the road of depression as one had advanced on that of expansion. Black Friday, 1929, gave the first warning of the impending crisis which in successive waves was to spread throughout the United States and to every country in Europe. The Great Depression should have signaled that something was basically wrong with a system that permits such a catastrophe to occur at all.[2]

If the gold standard is allowed to function freely, it is bound to be effective, since the momentum it sets up to bring things back into balance will not cease until equilibrium is actually restored. The gold standard, therefore, governs all the components of domestic and international transactions with faultless effectiveness.

Capitalism, in general, and the gold standard, in particular, tend to maintain the perpetuation of the economic system. And in so doing, the gold standard, while it guides men's actions, respects their freedom of choice.[3]

---

[2]Jacques Rueff, *The Age of Inflation,* trans. by A. H. Meeus and F. G. Clarke (Chicago: Henry Regnery Company, 1964), pp. 7-8.

[3]*Ibid.,* pp. 40-42.

14

THREE VARIATIONS OF THE GOLD STANDARD

Originally the true gold standard, sometimes called the orthodox or classical or pure gold standard, was a "gold-coin standard." All paper money was backed one hundred per cent by gold and convertible into gold. Gold coins were actually in the cash holdings of the people, in addition to bank notes, checkbook money, and fractional coins. Paper was a money substitute payable on demand in gold coins. (From 1882 to 1933 the United States' currency was backed by gold coins. They were called "gold certificates"; the color of the back of the paper note was gold and at the bottom of the obverse side it said, "United States of America, Fifty Dollars, In Gold Coin Payable To The Bearer On Demand.") Since they were redeemable into gold, they represented definite quantities of the metal gold. Both gold coins and paper notes (money substitutes) were in circulation. Under the gold-coin standard, money was gold and gold was money.

Since the beginning of this century, however, governments have undermined the gold standard. From the gold-coin standard, where the people had actual possession of gold coins as the circulating medium of exchange, governments gradually established the "gold-bullion standard," which afforded greater leeway for inflation and familiarized the people with paper money. The people innocently trusted the paper which was theoretically, but not in practice, as good as gold. Under this standard the government managed the gold bullion. Since gold coins were confiscated in the United States in 1933, they were no longer in circulation, and were accumulated in the vaults of central banks. The national currency was no longer redeemable in gold coins by United States citizens, but convertibility was retained between governments.

The gold standard was further eroded by the "gold-exchange standard." Governments began holding their country's gold reserves not in actual gold, but in foreign claims to gold, i.e., dollars and pounds were redeemable in gold, so central banks held paper dollars and paper pounds that were supposedly "as good as gold." By making only two currencies redeemable in gold, the world's monetary gold was gradually accumulated in a few central banks, which eventually became the reserve banks of the world.

After World War II the Bank of England and the United States Federal Reserve System controlled most of the world's stock of monetary gold; the United States controlled almost $24.5 billion in gold out of a total $40 billion gold. More than sixty nations held their reserves in pound sterling claims to gold, forming the sterling area. Twenty nations, mainly in Latin America, constituted the dollar area. But the Bank of England, in turn, held most of its reserves in dollar claims to gold, which made the Federal Reserve System the ultimate reserve bank of the world. Thus, the gold-exchange standard was reduced to a "de facto" dollar-exchange standard.

During the 1960s, the decade of the New Frontier and the Great Society, while social programs were being paid by the mushrooming money supply of the United States, the dollar fell from its position of predominance. Several monetary crises and runs on the British pound, which triggered worldwide demands for dollar redemption, greatly depleted the gold reserves of the United States and thus created precarious payment situations. In 1968, the United States gold supply stood at approximately $11 billion, while foreigners held over 35 billion "convertible" dollars. The next step signalled the end was near. In March, 1968, most governments joined the United States and put an embargo on gold payments and halted gold redemption of their currencies. This act amounted to a declaration of bankruptcy of the United States treasury, the international monetary "dollar-exchange standard," and, in fact, of all the individual currencies which took part in this gold-dollar scheme. This was the end of the gold-exchange standard and the beginning of the "fiat standard," which is no standard at all.

Although the gold standard produced price stability for 146

years, the period of the greatest economic growth of any nation in the history of the world, this price stability was an obstacle to government expansion and price manipulation. Therefore, the gold standard was under continual attack, until 1933, when it eventually succumbed to government intervention. From 1933 onward, Americans, and from 1968 onward, foreigners, have been plagued with endless inflation.

In 1968, the gates were flung wide open for worldwide inflation. Governments were going to play it "deuces wild." From that point on there has been no legal or procedural restraint of any kind, domestically or internationally, on the unlimited printing and spending of paper dollars by the United States government—nor on the paper money printing and spending of any other government that accepts paper dollars as "reserve assets"—that were once, a long time ago, as good as gold.

15

INFLATION OR THE GOLD STANDARD

The politicians were quick to take advantage of their new-found spending power—a power that seemed to allow them to increase government spending (usually popular) without increasing taxes (always unpopular). Although there were no legal limits to the United States government's deficit spending (deliberately spending more than one earns), there still remained one economic limit, a remnant of the gold standard. There existed a domestic tie between the dollar and gold—a "legal requirement" that the Federal Reserve "maintain" gold reserves against its notes and other liabilities (with no domestic obligation to pay them out). But politicians being politicians, they overcame the obstacle.

For 140 years (prior to 1934), the United States dollar was an honored promise to pay on demand .77 ounces of silver or .05 ounces (1/20th ounce) of gold, a ratio of sixteen to one. The plain language of the Constitution defines "lawful money" as gold or silver and *prohibits any governmental body from naming anything else money.* It assigned only a restricted power to Congress to "regulate the value" of the dollar, i.e., to change the definition of its weight in silver or gold. In 1934, following a ten-month gold embargo, President Roosevelt by edict changed the value of the dollar in gold to .028 ounces (1/35th ounce), leaving the value in silver unchanged at .77 ounce, creating a new silver/gold monetary ratio of twenty-seven to one.

At the same time as this first "devaluation" of the dollar, Congress passed the Gold Reserve Act of 1934. It terminated circulation of gold coins and free convertibility of the paper currency into gold for United States citizens and prohibited them from holding gold (except for rare coins) in the United States— a prohibition that President Eisenhower extended in the 1950s to holding gold abroad. The only remaining domestic link between the dollar and gold was an inconsequential carry-over from early days—a requirement that the Federal Reserve maintain gold reserves against its notes and other liabilities.

Initially, in the thirties, the requirement set these reserves at forty per cent against notes and thirty-five percent against other liabilities. But in practice, the legal reserve requirement was quite meaningless because each time the paper money supply was inflated to the legal limit, the legal minimum reserve limit was reduced. In 1945, the reserve requirement was reduced to twenty-five per cent on both notes and liabilities. In 1965, the reserve requirement against liabilities was abolished. In 1968, the twenty-five per cent gold reserve requirement against Federal Reserve notes in circulation was dropped by an act of Congress. The last legal restraint on the unlimited printing of paper dollars was thus removed.

Removal of the gold reserve requirement for Federal Reserve notes (your paper money) eliminated the last barrier to inflating continually the Nation's purchasing media. As long as a substantial gold reserve was required by law, the money-credit managers were confronted with a restraining influence.

Now, only the wisdom and determination of the Nation's money-credit managers can prevent the ultimate decline of the buying power of the dollar until it becomes nearly worthless. To what extent the citizens can rely on the wisdom and courage of those "responsible men" can be judged by events of the past three decades, including loss of two-thirds of the buying power of savings and life insurance, the increasing rate of depreciation in recent years, loss of much of the Nation's gold, and the fact that several of those managers have been among the most persistent in advocating the removal of all restraints. Truly wise and responsible men would not want to be without the guidance of such an objective criterion as a gold reserve requirement; and unwise, irresponsible men should not be relied upon to act properly without such guidance.

Judging by the foregoing, the dollar appears doomed to

continue losing buying power, the only question being: How long before it will be practically worthless?[1]

In fact, no currency in history has lasted more than forty-two years after its intrinsic value has been abandoned.[2]

The runaway deficit spending by the United States government in the 1960s has created a runaway inflation in the 1970s. The "federal debt" in 1960 was $290.9 billion; by 1970 it was $382.6 billion. That is $91.7 billion or a thirty-one per cent increase in the federal debt in only ten years. Federal tax revenues in the seven years from 1965 to 1972 increased sixty-eight per cent from $117 billion to $198 billion, while in the same period, outlays soared one hundred per cent, from $118 billion to $236 billion.[3]

Yes, the politicians were quick to act upon their ill-gotten gains (spending power). The two to three per cent inflation of the early sixties accelerated to five to six per cent inflation in the late sixties, and the seventies are faced with nine to ten per cent inflation, or worse. At ten per cent annual inflation, the currency depreciates one hundred per cent every ten years, or more precisely, prices double every ten years, or less.

The effects of inflation on the fixed income groups—retired people, those on annuities, pensions, or social security, the poor, and the needy—are inhuman. For instance, a man who retired as little as five years ago has witnessed twenty-five per cent inflation. How can a person plan for his retirement under such circumstances? If a man of forty-five today wishes to plan for his retirement twenty years hence, he must figure that since $10,000 is reasonable today, he will need $30,000 to $40,000 then. This is the logical outcome. This is the future which socialist paper money advocates have arranged for every citizen. A life of productive

[1]American Institute Counselors, Inc., in their *Investment Bulletin,* April 17, 1972.

[2]Newell H. Leppert, *Gold: The Natural Enemy of Socialism* (California: California Mining Journal, n.d.).

[3]Economic Research Corp., *Market Perspective,* June 7, 1972, V, 2, p. 3.

work is rewarded with an old age of poverty and degradation. It is already difficult for an elderly person to avoid becoming a ward of the state; in the future it will be virtually impossible. And pity the unfortunate person who is long-lived. An entire lifetime's energy and wealth will have been inflated beyond any value. His life and his money—especially his money—will seem worthless. He will be bewildered and demoralized. Inflation is nothing short of cruel, inhuman, and barbaric.

Is this always the final outcome of inflation? Yes. Must inflation always exist, embezzling the individual's hard-earned money, savings, and plans for the future? No!

Socialist governments, eager to stay in power, to spend other people's money, to rob Peter to pay Paul, to think up nonprofitable schemes that waste the taxpayer's money, who always seem to know what to do, but in reality, do not, socialists of all persuasions, have systematically sabotaged and destroyed the only objective standard and protection the individual has for his earnings and savings. The gold standard did not fail—it was assassinated.

Under the gold-coin standard, hereafter called the gold standard, inflationary policies are not rendered impossible, but made difficult. The gold standard is not a perfect or ideal standard. But Ludwig von Mises points out that nobody is in a position to tell us how something more satisfactory could be put in place of the gold standard.

The gold standard means sound money; it makes the value of money independent of government. It is true that the purchasing power of the gold is unstable. But the idea of stability and unchangeability of purchasing power is absurd. In a living, changing world there can be no such thing as stability of purchasing power. It is an essential feature of money that its purchasing power is changing. In fact, the adversaries of the gold standard do not want to make money's purchasing power stable, they want government to have the power to manipulate purchasing power, i.e., wages, prices, and interest rates, without being hindered by the will of the consumer.

Socialists' main objection to the gold standard is that the determination of prices is out of the control of government. There is an "external" or "automatic" force that restrains government's monetary power—the vicissitudes of gold production. Since the production of gold depends on its profitability, like all commodities, the significance of the gold standard is that the supply of gold limits the government's power to resort to inflation. The gold standard makes the purchasing power of money independent of the ambitions, whims, and doctrines of political parties and pressure groups. This is not a defect of the gold standard; it is its main excellence.

Every method of manipulating purchasing power is by necessity arbitrary and harmful to the market. For example, if government forces prices above the market level, surpluses result; if government forces prices below the market level, shortages result; if government forces prices to remain at the market level, its function is superfluous. The gold standard removes from government control the power to tamper with money's purchasing power.

To accept this concept, one must acknowledge the fact that government cannot make all the people richer by printing money. The abhorrence of the gold standard is inspired by the superstition that omnipotent governments can create wealth out of little scraps of paper. The gold standard cannot totally stop inflation; but it can check large-scale destructive inflationary ventures on the part of governments; and it can prove a safe haven for one's money while paper depreciates.

The gold standard protects the monetary system from the influence of government. A metallic money is not subject to government manipulation. The gold standard is an efficacious check upon credit expansion, as it forces the banks not to exceed certain limits in their expansionist ventures. Unconditional redemption keeps currencies at par with gold. The gold standard's own inflationary potentialities are kept within limits by the supply and demand of gold in the free market—the profitability of gold mining.

Under the gold standard, gold is money and money is gold, and the values of both are determined by the consumers' buying or abstention from buying on the free market.

Under laissez-faire capitalism, the government's monetary purpose has only one objective: to facilitate and to simplify the use of the medium of exchange which the people have chosen as money. Since a nation's currency system should be sound, the principle of soundness means that the coins should be properly assayed and the bars of bullion coined in such a way as to make the detection of clipping, abrasion, and counterfeiting easy. To the government's stamp no function is attributed other than to certify the weight and the fineness of the metal contained. (A function private enterprise can do cheaper.) Debased or worn coins are taken out of circulation and reminted.

During the California gold rush, private mints were established. The honesty and integrity of those mints were undeniable. Coins of those early private mints today are selling at substantial premiums and are some of the most prized specimens of notable coin collectors.

Without a gold standard to limit government spending, money substitutes eventually become worthless. Since the abandonment of the gold standard, the quantity of currency held by the public between 1933 and 1972 has risen from $5.5 billion to $66.6 billion, demand deposits from $13.5 billion to $178.6 billion, and time deposits from $21.8 billion to $309.3 billion. During this period the purchasing power of the dollar has fallen to merely pennies of the 1933 dollar. This is the result of the deadly disease of inflation.

Although inflation is a vicious form of taxation, it is popular to some people because its effects are rarely understood. There are the beneficiaries of inflation who sing loud praises of "easy money" and "credit expansion." The government and its economists invent intricate theories and doctrines to support their inflationary policies. For inflation boosts government revenue and permits politicians to spend more money than they can raise by taxes. Inflation, as it dilutes the value of the money supply, also repudiates government debt, at the expense of every working man.

In this respect, it is a silent tax on innocent money-owners and savers.

The government resorts to inflation because it dare not ask the taxpayers for more money to pay for its programs. If the circumstances were clearly laid before the taxpayers, government would have no chance of the consent of the people. The political function of inflation is obvious. Wars, giveaway programs, and public utilities are only a few examples of socialist schemes that require taxes to cover expenses and losses.

War, in particular, requires inflation. Financing wars by bank paper hides the true cost of the war from the voter. To fight a war is extremely costly. Under the gold standard, people are reluctant to incur such vast expenses. To circumvent this reluctance, wars have been financed by a more subtle method—inflation. People have been led to finance wars through subterfuge, and they still do not realize this fact. A study of history shows that an overwhelming majority of people would be unwilling to finance particular wars. And had America remained on the gold standard, it is unlikely that it would have been involved in most of the wars it has fought. Most people realize that neither side benefits from destruction.

Financing a war by paper money creates large profits for banks. Thus bankers constitute a powerful vested interest in favor of war. It is only in time of war that banks can create paper money in vast sums in order to lend it to needy governments. The history of several wars shows groups of bankers conspiring to bring about war. It is these same bankers who have influenced and made American foreign policy for the past sixty years—the sixty most warlike years in American history.

In addition, few people understand that inflation reduces the standard of living of all people. It diminishes the value of savings bonds, savings accounts, mortgages, life insurance policies, pensions, and other savings. It causes the economic instabilities of the trade cycle. And, above all, the losses which inflation inflicts on millions of people breed a political and economic radicalism that tends to destroy the private property order.

Only one man succeeded in coming to terms with inflation—

Hitler. He understood that inflation destroys the ties that bind
men to reality, and in so doing freedom threatens the social order.
To save the social order, he sacrificed freedom. By subjecting individual conduct to strict control, he restrained people from
utilizing that part of their purchasing power which exceeded the
value of purchasable wealth. In this way he was able to distribute
generously the means of buying goods which did not exist. He
turned this lie into a system of government.

Germany covered her financial deficits by creating paper
money and relying upon exceptionally severe controls to keep
prices from rising, as well as upon extended rationing to curb
the use of the excess purchasing power created by the deficit. All
Germans were supplied with plenty of money, but were kept from
spending it by draconian penalties—including the death sentence
—which also enforced rationing. Hitler's experience with inflation
was the natural outcome of economic tyranny. Such tyranny has
always resulted in the extinction of individual freedom. Rome
had Diocletian. Germany had Hitler.

Western civilization was founded on freedom, but it is doomed
to disappear unless it manages to break out of the inflationary
whirlpool where it is sinking relentlessly before our eyes. Who-
ever tolerates inflation but rejects disorder is a protagonist of
dictatorship.[4]

The capitalistic economy can only bear fruit under conditions
of stability. If it is to continue functioning it must rest again
on the firm monetary basis upon which it was erected. Today
after forty years of inflation, freedom can be saved by the re-
habilitation of money.[5]

The solution to the problem of inflation is simple—government should stop inflating. If that solution is too difficult to practice, then employ the gold standard to clean up the polluted money
supply. As Henry Hazlitt observed, gold means trust. It weighs
more and can be kept longer than a politician's pledge. And
nothing has more clearly demonstrated the need for the gold
standard than its abandonment, as the world has been plunged
into a sea of paper money and unending inflation.

---

[4]Reuff, *The Age of Inflation*, p. 69.
[5]*Ibid.*, p. 29.

16

DEPRESSION OR THE GOLD STANDARD

As soon as the inflation and credit expansion stop, the piper must be paid. The inevitable readjustments liquidate the unsound investments of the boom. Inflation must always lead to depression.

The correct but incomplete theory of depressions and the business cycle began with the eighteenth-century Scottish philosopher and economist David Hume. The work was continued by the eminent nineteenth-century English classical economist David Ricardo. The entire boom and bust theory, however, was not fully developed until the 1920s. The full explanation of the business cycle was developed by Ludwig von Mises in his monumental work, *Theory of Money & Credit,* published in 1912, and still, sixty-one years later, the best book on the theory of money and banking. By 1930, the great dean of monetary theory had discovered the complete phenomenon of the business cycle and the greatness of laissez-faire capitalism.

Business cycles are a natural phenomena in the free market. They originate from the functioning of supply and demand factors of products or commodities. Take gold, for example. If the supply is inadequate, the resulting shortage causes the price to rise. As the price rises, the mining of gold becomes more profitable and production increases. The higher the profit the more gold produced. Production continues until it becomes unprofitable to mine more gold. This occurs when supply equals demand and overtakes it. As demand subsides, the price falls. If and to the extent that production continues the price falls further. When the price has dropped to the level at which the production of more gold is unprofitable, production stops. Smart businessmen slow down their production as the price is falling, others go bankrupt. Production is curtailed to meet the lower demand.

Eventually the low production rate causes a shortage, forces up the price and the cycle begins again.

The business cycle occurs in all industries. Another example is the pig cycle.

> When the price for pork and bacon begins to rise at any given time, the immediate reflex of the farmer is to increase the breeding of pigs, to take advantage of the improved profit margins. Of course, each pig breeder thinks he's well ahead of everybody else in observing that great future profits must lie in this activity. But of course, he is not. Pig farmers all over the country, in search of future profits, borrow money and all start breeding pigs like crazy. Pigs being pigs, it takes about one and a half years for them to reach maturity from the word "go." And inevitably, at that point in time, the pig market is flooded. As a result of over-supply, prices begin to fall. The margin between sales price and cost of feed, etc., shrinks abruptly, so the pig farmers suddenly cut their pig breeding activities way back. All of them. In due course—measured again by Hanau (a German statistician) at one and a half years—a shortage of pigs develops in the market. Prices once again start to rise. The margin between prices and the cost of raising pigs widens, and the cycle begins anew.[1]

One of the beliefs today in economics, held both by private and government economists, is that the business cycle has been eliminated. This is false. As long as the means of production remain in the private sector and are based on the profit motive, there will be business cycles. An inherent feature of capitalism is that it is unstable. There is a continuous tendency for prices to move in one direction or another. The market is always seeking equilibrium, where supply equals demand, but changes of data, which are always taking place, prevent equilibrium from ever being reached.

These business cycles, of which there exist thousands, form

---

[1]Schultz, *Panics and Crashes*, p. 123.

an overall cycle. The overall cyclical behavior of an economy is the consequence of the combination and interaction of many small, interdependent cycles. This general economic cycle is known as the "boom and bust cycle."

Prior to World War I the boom and bust cycles were sharp and short-lived. Only certain segments of the economy were hit and then only on a short-term basis. The health of the whole economy was never in danger.

The reason for the milder cycles in the nineteenth century, the freest period in American history, was that government respected the efficacy of the free market. There was little government interference in the economy.

Why were the business cycles less severe then, and why did they get much worse?

In the nineteenth century, when the businessman-entrepreneur made an investment decision, he was spared the trouble of considering tax consequences, unions, consumer protectionists, ecologists, and wage and price controls. His entrepreneurial function rested solely on his judgment of whether or not his investment would be profitable. The better his judgment, the higher the profits he would earn. If his judgment overestimated the demand for his profit, he would suffer losses, and soon be forced out of business.

The market economy, therefore, is a profit and loss economy, in which the intelligence and ability of business entrepreneurs are gauged by the profits and losses they reap. The market contains a built-in mechanism that insures the survival and the flourishing of the most productive businessmen and the weeding out of the unproductive ones. For the more profits reaped by the successful businessmen, the greater become their business responsibilities and the more they will have available to invest in the productive system. On the other hand, a few years of making losses drive the unsuccessful entrepreneurs out of business. This profit and loss mechanism tends to keep businesses in the black and losses and business failures at a minimum.

The conclusion then is that the business cycle, by itself, is not capable of producing the severe inflation-depression cycle known in modern times. But what is it that causes the business world to suddenly experience severe and unaccountable losses?

The answer lies in another, but related, segment of the economy—in the money market. The money market originates in the institution of banking, with its capacity to expand credit and the money supply—first, in the form of paper money or bank notes, and later in the form of demand deposits or checking accounts, which are instantly redeemable in cash at the banks. It was the operations of commercial banks that held the answer to the extreme movements of the boom and bust cycle, which had puzzled observers since the mid-eighteenth century.

Dr. Murray Rothbard[2] explains how the boom and bust cycle gets its disruptive power from the banking system.

The natural moneys, gold and silver, are useful commodities. If money were confined to these commodities, then the economy would work in the aggregate, as it does in particular markets. There would be a smooth adjustment of supply and demand and, therefore, no boom and bust cycles. But the injection of bank credit adds a crucial and disruptive element.

Even though the money is backed by gold, banks can expand credit in the form of notes or deposits which are theoretically redeemable on demand in gold, but in practice are not. For example, if a bank has 1,000 ounces of gold in its vault, and it issues instantly redeemable receipts for 2,500 ounces of gold, and if there were no concerted pressure for redemption, the bank has been able to expand the money supply by 1,500 gold ounces.

The banks continue to expand credit, for the more they expand credit the greater their profits. As the money supply increases it bids up prices. The result is inflation and a boom within the country. The citizens naturally start to buy more goods from other countries where prices are lower. And foreigners buy fewer goods in the inflated country. The results are trade and balance of payments deficits. By imports exceeding exports, money flows to foreign countries.

---

[2]Dr. Murray Rothbard, *Economic Depression: Causes & Cures* (Lansing, Michigan: Constitutional Alliance, Inc., n.d.), pp. 13-18.

Foreigners, having no need for foreign paper money, present the money for redemption in gold. Thus gold is the type of money that flows persistently out of the country which has the inflation. During this period the banks have continued inflating, placing perhaps 4,000 ounces of gold receipts in circulation while the gold base has dwindled to, say, 800. Eventually the banks lose their nerve, because they are obligated to redeem those notes, stop their credit expansion and in order to save themselves, contract their outstanding bank loans.

The bank contraction reverses the boom and the bust follows. The fall in the supply of bank money leads to a general fall in prices. Goods become cheaper and competitive again. The balance of payments reverses itself and gold flows back into the country. As bank money contracts on top of an expanding gold base, the condition of the banks again becomes sound.

This, then, is the meaning of the depression phase of the business cycle. Note that it is the preceding inflation that makes the depression phase necessary. It is the process by which the economy throws off the excesses of the boom and reestablishes a sound economic condition. When the banks are in a confident position to resume their natural path of credit expansion, the cycle repeats itself.

The point here is that the boom-bust cycle is brought about, not by the free market economy, but by the banking system. The banks can only expand in unison when a central bank exists, essentially a government business, and a privileged position imposed by government monopoly over the entire banking system. If banks were truly competitive, any credit expansion by one bank would quickly pile up the debts of that bank in its competitors, who would quickly call for redemption. In short, a bank's rivals will call upon it for redemption in gold or cash in the same way as do foreigners, except that the process is much faster and would nip any incipient inflation in the bud.

By systematic intervention, government is the ultimate cause of bank expansion and inflation, and when the inflation comes to an end, the subsequent depression-readjustment comes into play.

Without bank credit expansion, supply and demand tend toward equilibrium through the free price system; no cumulative booms and busts can develop.

The pouring of new loan funds into the business community triggers another disruptive element which will eventually collapse the entire economy: the interest rate in the free market is artificially lowered. The result of "cheap money," the Misesian theory of the business cycle explains, causes the eventual and sudden cluster of business failures and the capital goods market to be hit harder than the consumer goods market.

Here is how it works. Businessmen, seeing the rate of interest fall, assume the public is saving and investing more money. They react as they always would and must to such a change of market signals: they expand their investment in durable equipment, in capital goods, in industrial raw material, in construction, as compared to their direct production of consumer goods. In short, businessmen react exactly as they would react if savings had genuinely increased. They happily borrow the cheap and abundant money.

As they invest in capital goods—machines, equipment, industrial plants—the money filters through the economy and wages and prices are bid up. The inflationary boom continues as long as money remains cheap. The longer it continues the wider the distortions of the pricing and production system.

When the banks get into a shaky condition or the public balks at the continuing inflation, the bank credit expansion finally stops.

Then the consumers reestablish their consumption/investment ratio. It is then revealed that business had invested too much in capital goods and had underinvested in consumer goods. The prices of labor and raw materials in the capital goods had been bid up during the boom too high to be profitable once the consumers reasserted their preferences. Business had been tricked, by the government's money policy, into thinking that more savings were available to invest than were really there.

The "depression" is then seen as the necessary and healthy phase by which the market liquidates the unsound, unprofitable investments of the boom, and reestablishes the consumption/investment ratio actually desired by the consumers. The depression is painful, but necessary. The prices of labor and goods in the capital goods industries must be allowed to fall until proper market relations are resumed.

According to Mises, the blame rests on the inflationary bank credit expansion propelled by the intervention of government and its central bank. The solution, says Mises, is that government must stop inflating.

It is true that this will, inevitably, bring the inflationary boom abruptly to an end, and commence the necessary recession or depression. But the longer the government waits for this, the worse the necessary readjustments will have to be. The sooner the readjustment is gotten over with, the better.

This means that government must never try to prop up or lend money to unsound businesses, never prop up wage rates or prices and never try to inflate again. Doing this will prolong the agony and convert a sharp, quick depression phase into a lingering and chronic disease, resulting in mass unemployment in the vital capital goods industries. The government must do nothing to encourage consumption; it must not increase its own expenditures, for this will further increase the social consumption/investment ratio. In fact, cutting the government budget will improve the ratio. What the economy needs is not more consumption spending, but more saving, in order to validate some of the excessive investments of the boom.

Thus, what the government should do, according to Mises, is absolutely nothing. It should, from the point of view of economic health and ending the depression as quickly as possible, maintain a strict hands off, "laissez-faire" policy. Anything it does will delay and obstruct the adjustment process of the market; the less it does, the more rapidly will the market adjustment process do its work, and sound economic recovery ensue.

The Misesian prescription is the exact opposite of the Keynesian: It is for the government to keep absolute hands off the economy, and to confine itself to stopping its own inflation, and to cutting its own budget.[8]

---

[8]*Ibid.*, pp. 25-26.

To sum up, whenever a free market economy exists, business cycles will occur. Business cycles are the normal functioning of the factors of supply and demand. It is the business cycle that renders the free market the most efficient means of satisfying consumer demands.

When the business cycle corrects itself, it is the natural process by which it throws off the excesses of the previous "boom" cycle. Since there are thousands of products in the marketplace, there are thousands of cycles. Since cycles run independently and at different lengths to each other, some are booming while others are busting. This keeps the economy on a steady path of progress. There is never a danger of upsetting the entire economy.

When government tampers with the market, it upsets the natural balance of the business cycle. By increasing the supply of money or expanding credit, it stimulates the entire economy with its cheap money policy. When the liquidating depression takes over, a would-be local depression spreads throughout the business world, causing the entire economy to collapse.

According to Mises, the government should then step out of the picture and let market forces straighten out the mess. This way the depression is quick and sharp and the economy can get back to the business of business. But government by nature is meddlesome: it tries to solve the very problem it created. It thus converts a short, healthy recession into a lingering and chronic depression.

This was the story of the Great Depression of the 1930s. The truth is that the Depression was not a result of laissez-faire capitalism which socialists are so eager to accuse. The 1929 crash was made inevitable by the vast inflationary policies of the Western governments during the 1920s, a policy deliberately adopted by all Western governments, including the Federal Reserve System. The depression that followed the crash was also inevitable. Its long duration was not. The deliberately adopted programs and controls and government meddling kept the economy in a constant state of uncertainty and confusion. Market forces could not right themselves. Government interference prolonged the depression. For the first time in American history, there existed a nearly perpetual depression and nearly permanent mass unemployment.

The debacle of the Great Depression was a result of the failure of the Western governments to return to the gold standard after World War I.

Instead of returning to the gold standard, which would have deflated most postwar economies, especially England's, the "gold-exchange standard" was adopted. The gold-exchange standard enabled countries to back their currency not only with gold, but with dollars or sterling, which were supposedly convertible into gold. The gold-exchange standard worked in such a way that when money left one country it added purchasing power to the second country, while leaving the purchasing power of the first country intact, creating a duplication of purchasing power. Since capital flowed without gold payments following, the gold-exchange standard postponed the simple correction that the gold standard would have realized. Consequently, the gold-exchange standard was one of the main causes of the inflationary boom that lasted until 1929, when the day of reckoning came.

Every experience with irredeemable paper money in America's history has failed. And all the while the malicious boom/bust cycle is demolishing the hard work of American industry—of private initiative and enterprise. Every scheme with cheap money has hurt the public welfare. And the cost has been more than a purely specie currency would have cost, if each generation had had to buy it anew.

To paraphrase Professor William Graham Sumner, the great Yale economist of the pre-Federal Reserve era, a new gold-coin standard could be established every year out of the depreciation losses suffered by the millions of honest productive men in society. And the needed gold could be purchased again and again from the losses suffered by the millions of victims of a depression. Indeed, the gold-coin standard is a bargain price for economic stability.[4]

---

[4]Sennholz, *Inflation or Gold Standard?*, p. 18.

17

FALLACIES ABOUT THE GOLD STANDARD

Although some people trust in the efficacy of the gold standard, they argue against its establishment because they believe it is either irrational, immoral, or impractical. There are ten main fallacies about the gold standard that prevent Americans from giving it the support it deserves. Once these fallacious beliefs are eliminated by reason, logic, and facts, support of the gold standard can spread nationwide.

The first fallacy is that gold is mystical; people are drawn to gold because of some mysterious, irrational, irresistible charm. And if governments did not use gold for monetary purposes the price of gold would be much less than it is. But in reality, when the United States closed the gold window in August, 1971, gold was selling around $43 an ounce. One year later it sold for $65 an ounce, a fifty per cent increase. Two years later it sold for $120 an ounce, a hundred per cent increase. It seems that whenever governments fight the individual's choice to own gold, gold sells at a premium. But when governments respect the individual's choice, the price of gold stabilizes and the premium disappears.

Actually, people are attracted to gold for very good reasons. Gold has many uses in industry, and as money, it is par excellence. Those who see no value in gold are blind to reality. Gold is rational and scientific. Gold is not mystical. The real mystical idea is that by proclaiming the magic words "legal tender," the divine right of kings enables the high priest of the state (the secretary of the treasury) to make a worthless piece of paper into a thing of value. It is not the idea of objective value which is mystical; it is the idea of something for nothing, the idea that wealth can be created by printing pieces of paper, which is mystical. How can paper, specifically a two and a half inch by six inch piece of United States currency, whose industrial value is a small fraction of a cent, acquire a value of one dollar? And worse, how can the same piece of paper become worth one hundred or one thousand dollars merely by changing the numbers inked on its face? Gold is real; it has objective value to people, and its market value is determined by free exchange, not by the pronouncement of a higher authority via a procedure unknown to the general public.[1]

The second fallacy is that the gold standard is old-fashioned. Because something has been effective for a long period of time does not make it old-fashioned. In fact, it is its dependability that necessitates its perpetuation. To the extent man requires a code of values to guide his thoughts and actions, he requires a standard of value to guide his monetary judgments. Unchanging principles such as those of the Founding Fathers' are not old-fashioned. What are "good" and "right" are always fashionable. The value of money should always be kept stable, backed by the honesty and integrity, i.e., the gold reserves of the government or the bank issuing the money. Gold is progressive and advanced, and should be properly regarded as the vanguard of the future. In the words of Jacques Rueff, the famous French economist, "Tomorrow, to save man, we will give him a real currency."[2]

The third fallacy is that the gold standard is severe and inhuman. But just the opposite is true. It is paper money, inflation, which oppresses the poor. It is paper money that robs the poor and middle classes. Daniel Webster, in 1832 on the floor of Congress denounced printing press money as the deceit it is.

> Of all the contrivances for cheating the laboring classes of mankind, none have been more effectual than that which deludes them with paper money. This is the most effectual of inventions to fertilize the rich man's field by the sweat of the poor man's brow. Ordinary tyranny, oppression, excessive taxation . . . these bear lightly on the happiness of the mass of the community compared with fraudulent currencies and the robberies committed by depreciated paper.

---

[1] Howard S. Katz, *Committee to Reestablish the Gold Standard,* 85 Fourth Avenue, Suite 6M, New York, New York, 10003.

[2] Rueff, *The Age of Inflation,* p. 85.

It is unlimited paper money that yields huge profits to banks who issue endless amounts of credit. And the losers are the rest of the community because the created money claims real goods, which are bid up in price or no longer available to the community which produced them in the first place. The gold standard stands in the way of this insidious process. It serves justice and humanity.

The fourth fallacy is the idea that gold can be replaced by "paper gold" or Special Drawing Rights (SDRs). This flight of fancy is the invention of Keynesian economists, who believe that abstract ideas are more important than reality. Since real gold is scarce and expensive, their ideal is paper gold. Their idea of gold is an abstraction, and abstractions can be created out of nothing. (Something for nothing again.) But as Donald J. Hoppe points out, there is one difficulty: abstract ideas are like soap bubbles; when they are touched they disappear. SDRs are based on the same abstraction as the money of the United States—Federal Reserve notes. Although SDRs are defined in terms of gold they can never actually be redeemed in gold.

> They are intended forever to remain abstractions—evidences of debt that can never be repaid. Money is to be debt and debt is to be credit, and the debt is evidenced by interest-bearing notes or bonds. When due, the principle and the interest on the bonds are paid from the proceeds raised by the sale of more bonds. The more we get into debt the richer we are to become.[8]

This is the theory of paper gold. It is the most mystical and irrational of all ideas. The United States government can force its citizens to accept inconvertible, worthless, paper money, but it cannot force other nations to accept it. Since SDRs create additional liquidity in international trade, and since at the moment, there is too much liquidity in foreign central banks, as evidenced by worldwide inflation, SDRs will remain out of

---

[8]Hoppe, *How to Invest in Gold Coins*, p. 55.

favor with those who deal with reality. The world needs no more paper; it needs more stability—that means gold.

The fifth fallacy is that an increase in the price of gold would benefit only South Africa and Russia, and the United States should not support any country which supports slavery. Regarding South Africa, there is no slavery. The blacks work, not by force, but voluntarily. They receive higher wages in the gold mines than they would receive working in the jungle. Regarding Russia, there is slave labor. All labor is slave labor; there is no freedom. But since the United States government has made trade with Russia acceptable and has even encouraged it, there is no reason why a higher gold price cannot be supported. In addition, if the United States does not want to help Russia's gold mining industry, then why were millions of dollars worth of surface gold mining machinery shipped to Russia through San Francisco under the Lend-Lease program after the closing of most of the gold mines in the United States in 1942?[4] This enabled Russia to boost her gold mining production and at the same time permanently end gold production in the United States. In fact, a gold price rise would help the United States more than either Russia or South Africa. It would again make gold mining profitable in the United States, which would create half a million jobs and restore prosperity to many depressed communities. But above all, increasing gold production at home can save individual freedoms. Increasing gold production would make gold money available. It would stop deficit-spending, stop inflation, and reverse the nation's trend toward socialism and self-destruction. On balance, the United States by far would benefit most.

Fallacy number six is that in a major crisis the gold standard "breaks down." As proof, the example usually cited is that after World War I, when Great Britain returned to the gold standard, she had to abandon it six years later. The problem was that Britain suffered from wartime inflation; prices in Britain in 1924 were seventy per cent above their prewar level. But the British

---

[4]George Racey Jordan, *Gold Swindle: The Story of Our Dwindling Gold* (Los Angeles: The Bookmailer, Inc., 1959), p. 9.

government decided to resume the gold standard, in 1925, at the prewar and pre-inflation parity. Because the British were unwilling to make corresponding cuts in retail prices and wage rates, which would cut prices to the prewar level, the result was falling exports, stagnation, and unemployment. And it was the gold standard itself, not the false rate (or the internal inflexibility of wages), that got the blame. What Britain, and most governments, wanted the gold standard to do was to prop up their ailing currencies, to retain the old parity rate, to prevent the devaluation that was necessitated by the wartime inflation. They said their currencies were as good as gold and rendered inflation as invisible as the emperor's new clothes. But the public knew the truth. The currencies were heavily inflated beyond their gold reserves. The government should have let gold seek its own free market level and then resume convertibility. But that would have amounted to a devaluation of the pound, though economically correct, politically unpalatable. The result was a steady fall in wholesale prices from 1925 until September, 1931, when Britain abandoned the gold standard. It was the United States "helping" Britain retain the false prewar rate of $4.86 instead of insisting on the actual devalued rate that had sunk as low as $3.18 in February, 1920, that caused the Great Depression of the 1930s around the world, and also the abandonment of the gold standard by the United States in 1933. The gold standard did not break down; it was deliberately destroyed, and along with it the economies of the civilized world.

Fallacy number seven is the idea that the "fiat standard" is more workable than the "gold standard." "Fiat" is a polite word for "worthless." Worthless money can only work for planners and bureaucrats; it lets the servant become master. The fiat standard, by inflation, is the means by which governments expand and gain control of the people and their property. The debt standard sows the seeds of its own destruction. In fact, "From the days of ancient Rome, history reveals that any nation foolish enough to adopt fiat money has suffered an economic collapse, and many such nations have disappeared from the face of the earth. No currency in history has lasted more than 42 years after its intrinsic base has been abandoned."[5] The fiat standard goes with the welfare state; the gold standard goes with the private property state. Worthless money and the welfare state go hand in hand down the path of self-destruction to oblivion. Strong money and the private property state go hand in hand up the path of prosperity, patriotism, and freedom. The gold standard prevents excessive inflation. Its unmanageability is its main excellence.

The eighth fallacy is that gold creates inflation. Socialists claim that raising the price of gold would create inflation. However, the price of gold was frozen in 1934 at $35 an ounce and the United States has suffered from inflation every year since. Inflation is caused by an increase in the supply of money and credit. It is government-created. Inflation is like a cancer; unless it is completely stopped, it will spread until it eventually kills the entity. Gold is an inflation-fighter. It destroys the cancer and renders the entity fit to live.

In a free market, the quantity of goods and services determines the price and production of gold. This way gold maintains the price stability of all commodities. Indeed, between 1850 and 1900 many prospectors must have wondered if the huge quantity of gold produced would push prices higher. But just the opposite happened; it stimulated world production of all goods. As George Bernard Shaw said, ". . . With a gold currency it tends to maintain itself even when the natural supply of gold is increased by discoveries of new deposits, because of the curious fact that the demand for gold in the world is practically infinite . . ." Futhermore, during the 146 years from the establishment of the gold standard in 1787 until it was abandoned in 1933, the price level remained stable. Wholesale prices in 1787 were approximately the same as they were 146 years later. This remarkable feat was the result of a stable currency and capitalism, which has a tendency toward lowering the price level of commodities. The record shows that the gold standard has proven itself in its ability to fight inflation; no other monetary system has.

---

[5]Leppert, *Gold: The Natural Enemy of Socialism.*

The ninth fallacy is: it is a waste of money and energy to dig up gold from one place simply to bury it again in another place. This is partially true. Nevertheless, money managers have proven that they cannot be trusted to keep the value of money sound. By its demented economic and fiscal policies of the last three decades, the United States has forfeited all confidence in its ability to maintain the value of its currency. Therefore, it is certainly no waste of money and energy to dig up gold and bury it again if that process keeps the paper money sound and inflation a thing of the past. More importantly, gold should be dug up to be spent. It should be dug up, minted, and spent—put into circulation. Gold is good, hard, instant money. What better reason for mining it?

The tenth and final fallacy about the gold standard is that there is not enough gold available to use it for money. This is true. The reasons for the shortage are three: First, the gold mines in the United States were forced to shut down in 1942 by order No. L-208. This action, for all practical purposes, totally destroyed the gold mining industry in the United States. For whenever a mine is closed, the tunnels fill with water, the supports rot, and the machinery rusts. The damage inflicted upon the mining industry was tremendous, and to this day, the government has never made an offer to reimburse any of the mine owners. The second reason is price control. Gold has been under strict price control since 1934 when the price was frozen at $35 an ounce. Whenever a price control forces a price below the market level it creates a profit-squeeze. With endless inflation causing the costs of mining to rise four to five times their 1940 level, it is no wonder why gold is unprofitable to mine in the United States. Price control is the problem; a free gold market is the solution. The third reason for the gold shortage is hoarding. Whenever people lose confidence in their government and in their currency, they hoard the real, hard money—gold. Consequently, gold coins and gold bullion (where allowed) have been hoarded for decades. Recently, gold hoarding has accelerated as all paper money in the world is suspect.

A renaissance in gold thinking would reverse this trend, and the confidence it would produce in the public's mind would release this gold from hiding. As in the Byzantine Empire, where gold flowed freely, the United States and the rest of the world would once again be adequately supplied with gold.

A higher gold price would be the incentive to find new discoveries. There is even talk of reclaiming gold from the ocean. But there is plenty of gold closer to home and cheaper to mine in the continental United States, especially in California. According to the Division of Mines, over *20,000* gold mines are closed in California alone. Jack Sheedy, owner of the Telegraph mine in Downieville, California, said, "There is more gold left in California than ever was taken out." In the Mother Lode of California, there are only two mines that go below a mile in depth. The others have never been mined below the 2,500 foot level. Yet the formation is the same. The two deeper mines paid off every foot of the way, and many engineers claim that this area alone has the potential of South Africa.[6] In testimony before a House committee a few years ago, some engineers' reports showed that only ten per cent of the available gold supply has ever been removed from the earth.

When Captain Leppert was elected President of the Western Mining Council, he made a conscientious effort to do something about reopening the gold mines. Most of the gold mining areas in the United States are depressed areas, and the reopening of these mines would require 50,000 miners alone. Since it requires ten workers in other occupations to support a gold miner, this would create half a million jobs, and would remove the "depressed area" label from many communities. Captain Leppert discovered something else: "The gold mines in the United States are closed because somebody in Washington wants them closed."[7] The effect of this policy has become obvious to most Americans. It is dangerous to national security and to the economy. Senator Byrd once said that the gold drain (from the U.S. Treasury) was more of a threat to the security of our nation than the atomic

---

[6]*Ibid.*
[7]*Ibid.*

bomb. The security of any nation is the number one responsibility of its government. Therefore, restoration of the gold standard should be government's number one priority.

Actually, there is more gold per capita now than ever before. The greatest era of gold production in history has occurred thus far in the twentieth century. There are untold billions in gold-ore reserves waiting to be mined, as soon as it becomes profitable to do so. There is more than enough gold to reestablish a full international gold standard, *if it were properly used,* as a balancing wheel for international trade. There is, and always has been enough gold to finance balanced international trade. There will never be enough gold—or anything else—to finance policies of unrestrained deficits.[8]

Gold is the natural enemy of socialism. And there is no good reason why Americans cannot be fully armed (with gold) and protected (by gold) against socialism—the most dangerous threat to their life, liberty, and property.

---

[8]Donald J. Hoppe, *How to Invest in Gold Stocks and Avoid the Pitfalls* (New York: Arlington House, 1972), p. 184.

18

HOW TO RETURN TO THE GOLD STANDARD

It is of prime importance to Americans to return to the gold standard. It is the only protection an individual has against economic tyranny—inflation, taxation, and confiscation.

Under the current monetary system the value of the dollar is determined, not by the amount of gold or the amount of goods produced, but by the politicians in power. This arbitrary power to issue debt currency must be stopped. Freedom in America means a return to sound monetary policies. That means the reestablishment of the gold standard. This can be accomplished without much ado, and several economists have made the appropriate recommendations. The general principles of the following plan on how to return to the gold standard are taken from Alden Rice Wells' article, "Spending Money,"[1] which together with its supporting materials is being sponsored for a Nobel Prize in Economics. There is, perhaps, no single American more qualified to advocate the needed reforms to our monetary system than Alden Wells. He is one of the few persons who has a thorough understanding of the Federal Reserve System. He has warned that unless fundamental reform of the money system is accomplished, the United States is headed for deflation, bank failures, and a depression of severe proportions, along with it its social consequences, perhaps revolution. This plan is designed to eliminate the instabilities of the present monetary system, and to restore money to something of value.

Since economic order breeds political order, time is of the essence.

Good spending money is the vital element in domestic tranquility. As government has taken it upon itself to furnish the

---

[1]Alden R. Wells, *Alden R. Wells Quarterly*, Exeter, New Hampshire, October, 1972.

country with a medium of exchange, it is required by law to furnish a good spending money. That means gold and silver. It will do no good for government to blame the declining purchasing power of the dollar on speculators, profiteers, labor, business, or bankers, since it is the sole issuer and regulator of the money supply. To face reality is a step toward the solution.

It is not enough to permit citizens to own gold while forcing them to use only government paper money as the legal tender. Europeans have the right to own gold, and they suffer from runaway inflation. In order to stop currency depreciation, citizens must have the right to refuse the use of government money and the right to choose any commodity they wish to use.

Today, therefore, the first step toward sound money is to remove *all* restrictions on buying, selling, owning, and trading gold from American citizens. This means United States citizens can own gold in the United States or anywhere else in the world, in any form they wish and without any discriminatory tax. To further insure this all-important step, the legal tender laws should be repealed. This would free Americans from monetary bondage and give back to them a Constitutional right. Only in communist and socialist countries, where monetary freedom is prohibited, are such restrictions in force.

In this first period of the reform it is imperative that the United States government and all institutions dependent upon it, including the Federal Reserve System and Treasury, keep entirely out of the gold market. A *free* gold market could not come into existence if the government were to try to manipulate the price by underselling, or by imposing a discouraging tax, of, say, thirty-three per cent. The new monetary system must be protected against malicious acts on the part of the officials of the Treasury and the Federal Reserve System. There cannot be any doubt that officialdom will be eager to sabotage a reform whose main purpose it is to curb the power of the bureaucracy in monetary matters.

Gold money and government money would circulate side by side. This would prevent a severe deflation in the money supply, wages, and prices. Gold could be deposited in a bank for a receipt. Banks would become financially sound. The competition would also strengthen government money, as it would break up the monopoly that government holds over the money supply. The power of the Federal Reserve System—the central bank—would be ended. It would be unable to further inflate the money supply and finance wars and welfare programs.

The second step is to allow private citizens to mint gold coins for monetary use. With no legal tender or dollar/gold ratio the coins should be minted by weight only—one ounce, half ounce, quarter ounce, eighth ounce. Since an ounce of gold is always an ounce of gold, the marketplace would determine the proper value of the coins. This would tend to stabilize prices for the first time in decades.

If the government wished to mint coins of good quality—gold and silver—it could do so. And the profit it makes from "making money" would be sharply reduced. For example, not long ago a silver quarter cost the government about twenty cents. Today its replacement, the base metal quarter, costs less than two cents. A one thousand dollar note cost pennies and the government can buy one thousand dollars worth of goods with it. This profit, or seigniorage, is the easiest method by which governments extract spending money from the people without it being noticed. The additional cost of gold and silver money would reduce the government's seigniorage substantially. The added value would be passed on to the people. Gold coins would again be in the cash holdings of the people, along with government money and checkbook money. The gold-coin standard would eliminate the costly and complex dealings between the Federal Reserve System, the banks, and the Treasury. It would eliminate the huge profit government earns by "making (printing) money." It would eliminate the horrible debt system which is behind the current monetary system. It would eliminate the enormous interest payments on that debt for which American taxpayers are paying.

The necessity of this is apparent. In 1946, the income of the Federal Reserve System was $104 million. Today it is $3.8 billion. Here is a vested interest and a determination to expand power unequaled by any other bureaucracy. A gold-coin standard would save American taxpayers $3.8 billion. It would also end a power-hungry bureaucracy.

There are three other powerful departments intent on building their own bureaucracies: the Treasury Department, the Bureau of the Budget, and the Council of Economic Advisors. Responsibility for United States financial affairs is divided among these four departments. No progress toward economic health is possible as long as responsibility is so divided; only confusion results. The Constitution, with cool reason, designated the Secretary of the Treasury as the officer in charge. As step number three, the other two competing departments should be abolished when the reform begins.

Power-hungry men can subvert the Constitutional safeguards, as they have proven; the curbs recommended here are more potent: (1) Restore an unrestricted gold system, which will provide the public and the banking system with the impetus to curb lavish governments; (2) end the Federal Reserve System, which will substantially reduce the banking system's instability.

During the past thirty years of inflation, deposits in commercial banks multiplied over sevenfold, while their capital increased less than threefold. Consequently, the protection capital affords depositors was cut by more than half. Inflation, as always, creates an apparent liquidity, but in reality an illiquidity. To rectify this precarious situation, step number four requires the banks to raise their capital to ten per cent of deposits, and, furthermore, seventy-five per cent of the capital must be in gold coins. Part of the coins will be supplied by all the Treasury's gold, which should be minted into one-ounce gold coins without par value or legal tender value. Transferring the Treasury's gold to the banks would free the government's gold reserve (which, after all, is the property of American citizens held in safekeeping) and put it to good use. This would unsterilize the gold supply. As the economy stands today, it is rigid and the only way it can respond to inflation is by continuing currency depreciation; this must stop.

Banks will need time, perhaps ten years, to raise their capital to the required ratio. In the meantime, the Federal Reserve should turn over to the Treasury all of the Treasury securities behind the deposits commercial banks maintain with it in exchange for gold coins at market value. In turn, those coins should be delivered to the banks in place of their deposits at the Federal Reserve, at the same price. The Treasury's debt would be reduced about $30 billion without economic effect. That would save the American taxpayer more than $1.5 billion in annual interest payments.

The fifth step requires that the banks should be given national charters permitting the opening of branches everywhere, provided no bank is allowed to acquire more than five per cent of the total deposits in the nation, capital reserves equal ten per cent of deposits and seventy-five per cent of the capital is gold.

The sixth step concerns the dollar's international relations. To keep a currency's parity rate fixed, governments must buy and sell their currency with reserves in money other than their own currency. The only universally acceptable money, because it can withstand war and inflation, is gold. As a result of a lack of gold, the parity of the dollar is undefendable. Therefore, the sixth step requires denouncing any attempt to recreate parities either for gold or the dollar. A completely free gold market is the only way to stabilize the currency. A good example of a free floating currency is the Canadian dollar. Since Canada unpegged her dollar, she has avoided the international monetary turmoil, which has been plaguing other currencies. The free market has effectively determined the value of the Canadian dollar. She neither defends nor supports her currency, and it has remained exceptionally stable.

A government-fixed parity is a price control. A parity set at any other price than the market price is undefendable and extremely costly to the treasury. The beneficiaries of the United States' effort to maintain a false parity have been foreigners. Foreign governments now own over fifty billion dollars worth of Treasury securities on which American taxpayers must pay more than 2.5 billion dollars tax-free interest annually. Foreigners also own sixty per cent of what was originally our gold.

The values of the dollar and of gold must be allowed to

seek their own level. They have been controlled in one way or another for over fifty years. No one can possibly know at what price gold should be selling. There is no magic or scientific formula. The marketplace, in time, can provide the answer.

It is time the United States put its house in order. Both reason and experience prove that the gold standard contributes to a greater stability in prices than exists under any other monetary standard. F. A. Hayek points out that in the United States, during the period 1749-1939, there does not seem to have occurred a significant upward trend of prices. Compared with this, the rate at which prices have risen during the last quarter century (during the dollar standard), represents a major change.

> To what extent the record can be described as one of "creeping inflation" or "chronic inflation" or "galloping inflation" or whatever, is somewhat beside the point. Since abandoning the traditional gold standard, the record certainly does not point to any appreciable deflationary influences in the long-run view. The upward movement of prices during the 20th century contrasts sharply with the period of effective functioning of the gold coin standard in the United States and Britain during the previous two centuries.[2]

The case for gold was effectively summarized by the National City Bank of New York in their Monthly Letter of December, 1951, on page 135:

> . . . Fluctuations in the buying power of money are familiar over all history. Gold has had the best record over the centuries as a store of value. Paper money has been good when issued by banks which have been under a legal obligation to maintain convertibility into gold at the option of the holder. The old pound sterling and the old U.S. dollar were currencies of this type; their very names become synonymous

---

[2]Arthur Kemp, *The Role of Gold* (Washington, D.C.: American Enterprise Institute for Public Policy Research, 1963), p. 35.

with enduring value. Paper money directly issued by National Treasuries has the worst record. . . .[3]

Henry Hazlitt said, "It is precisely when a free gold market is needed that most modern governments seek to suppress it. For it reflects and measures the extent of the lack of confidence in the domestic currency; and it exposes the fictitious quality of the 'official' rate. And these are among the very reasons why it is needed."[4]

This is where the United States is today. The International Monetary Fund, the London Gold Pool, Special Drawing Rights, the Federal Reserve System, the Council of Economic Advisers, the Bureau of the Budget, and Lord Keynes have all failed. Government has failed in its responsibility to maintain a strong currency. The only thing that can bring back economic stability is denounced and suppressed.

The gold standard is not the panacea. But in spite of the many criticisms leveled against it, it is difficult to prefer the alternative of managed paper money with its history of price inflation, money depreciation, and loss of individual freedoms. The gold standard was a lot better system than critics will admit. The so-called weaknesses of the gold standard can be attributed to things other than gold. By and large the gold standard has run into trouble only when governments interfere with the operations of the standard either domestically or internationally, or both. An automatic monetary mechanism such as the gold standard is decidely superior to arbitrary monetary powers in promoting economic stability.

The foregoing plan on how to return to the gold standard is a guide that can be followed on the road to economic stability and to ending inflation. There is no easy, simple, painless plan. The bill for the inflation of the last thirty years is coming due. The piper will be paid. But there is still a choice between paying it voluntarily by shrinking the money supply, deflating wages and

[3]*Ibid.*, p. 37.
[4]*Inflation*, pp. 56-57.

prices, getting rid of the excesses and starting anew on a solid foundation, where the people can be forewarned and prepared. Or the United States will face the inevitable depression which will surely come without warning, and come with a vengeance. No matter what happens, the question of the gold standard versus the paper standard will be solved soon—either under the pressure of emergency or with quiet deliberation. To wait for the emergency is to invite disaster. It cannot be allowed to be solved otherwise than with deliberation. To spare the American people the disorder and suffering of a crisis of cataclysmic proportions, the proper action must be taken as soon as possible.

Today, government is into everything except that in which it belongs. The court system, instead of trying appeals, is legislating by interpreting the Constitution, a legislative function. Defense spending, which should be number one priority, totals only one billion dollars more than it did ten years ago. And in that same decade, the cost of things that Americans can do for themselves—social programs—have soared 266 per cent from $30 to $110 billion. This cannot continue forever.

It is time to face reality and plan for the future. Only a plan, such as the foregoing, based on reality, can succeed. It is time to think first of the United States. Let the United States keep the remaining portion of the gold supply for itself—the part that has not been redistributed throughout the world—as a base from which to build a new, sturdy monetary system. (Besides, Europe has enough United States gold to start her own gold standard.) The example of the gold-coin standard can do more for the citizens of the United States and of the other nations than any self-sacrificing gestures. Americans have sacrificed enough. This is no time for sacrifices; this is a time for courage and integrity.

When the gold standard is reestablished, the future will be secure from the tyranny of devastating inflations and depressions. It is time the government respected private property. To stop inflation, demand gold. All Americans can unite on this stand.

19

GOLD GOES WITH FREEDOM

Down through the ages, the history of man has been one of tyranny and oppression. The periods of freedom during ancient Greece and Rome were brief. Freedom has been the exception. The true revolution for human freedom, the revolution of ideas, was the only new and glorious change that happened to the race of man in over 6,000 years of history. The founding of the United States of America was where man finally created the reality of individual freedom.

The degree of any country's freedom is the exact degree of its progress. America, the freest country, achieved the most. Americans owe their high standard of living to the economic system, which presupposes individual freedom and property rights —Capitalism.

Capitalism wiped out slavery in matter and in spirit. Capitalism leaves every man free to choose the work he likes, to specialize in it, to trade his product for the product of others, and to go as far on the road of achievement as his ability and ambition will carry him. The basic premise of the Founding Fathers was man's right to his own life, to his own liberty, and to the pursuit of his own happiness. The political implementation of this right is a society where men deal with one another as traders, by voluntary exchange to mutual benefit. To guarantee freedom to one individual requires that freedom be guaranteed to all individuals. Capitalism implements this guarantee.

The opposite of freedom is slavery. Socialism implements slavery by government planning. The experience of recent decades has shown repeatedly that inflation, an inherent part of a socialist society, has inevitably entailed comprehensive rationing, price and wage controls, compulsory distribution of the means of production (including labor), extensive import quotas, prohibition of foreign travel—in short, widespread control over individual freedom, culminating in the abolition of freedom itself.

The contrast between the two systems is clear. In planning, the individual takes orders. In the free price system, he exercises his freedom of choice. Thus two extreme types of society are placed in juxtaposition: the gloomy society obeying orders against its will, and the enthusiastic society where everyone does freely and voluntarily what he wants to do. The former system begets dreary poverty and the latter enthusiastic prosperity.

The free price mechanism can achieve in hours what socialist planning—although reinforced with dictatorial powers—will always fail to achieve, no matter how many years it tries. The free price system allows profit and, as David Ricardo rightfully said, "Nothing contributes so much to the prosperity and happiness of a country as high profits."

To want freedom without wanting the conditions that make it possible is to ask to be keenly disappointed. Individual freedom is the surest way to peace and prosperity. To implement the capitalistic society there must exist a sound monetary system. Sound money is truly the only road to a free and prosperous country.

Money, which is necessary to insure the peaceful and profitable exchange of goods and services and the fulfillment of contracts, must, if standards mean anything, be a unit of exchange of the highest quality and of universal validity. That means gold. Wherever gold has been permitted to perform its function as only a unit of gold convertibility can, it has insured economic stability and pride and a sense of security among the people, giving strength to the character of the nation itself. Gold embodies the element of integrity, without which no nation can lay just claim to leadership or true greatness.

Historically, the record of man's outstanding successes has been written when the monetary supremacy of gold was recognized and encouraged, and his most colossal failures have resulted from trying to manufacture the illusion of wealth from the promises and threats of government.

In his often quoted, but always appropriate piece of advice,

George Bernard Shaw summarized the importance of money and of gold:

> The most important thing about money is to maintain its stability so that a dollar will buy as much a year hence, or ten years hence, or fifty years hence as today, and no less. With paper money this stability has to be maintained by the Government. With a gold currency it tends to maintain itself even when the natural supply of gold is increased by the discovery of new deposits, because of the curious fact that the demand for gold in the world is practically infinite. You have to choose (as a voter) between trusting to the natural stability of gold, and the natural stability, and the honesty and intelligence of the members of the Government. And, with due respect to those gentlemen, I advise you, as long as the Capitalistic system lasts, to vote for gold.

Not heeding Shaw's advice, the United States abandoned the gold standard. Since the United States adopted socialism, it has suffered from two world wars, two "conflicts," and endless inflation. It has watched its youth torn between drugs and the draft. It has witnessed the moral decline of its citizenry. This is the shabby secret of the welfare-statists-socialists' tirades against gold. Inflation, via deficit-spending, is simply a nefarious scheme for the "hidden" confiscation of wealth, which enriches banks and pays for wars. Gold stands in the way of this insidious process. It stands as a protector of property rights and of life itself. It keeps the moral fiber of a country as strong and self-reliant as its money.

Ludwig von Mises warns that the struggle against gold, which is one of the main concerns of all contemporary governments, must not be looked upon as an isolated phenomenon. It is but one item in the gigantic process of destruction which is the mark of our time. People fight the gold standard because they want to substitute national autarky for free trade, war for peace, totalitarian government omnipotence for liberty.[1]

---

[1]*Human Action*, p. 476.

This is socialism—war instead of peace, arbitrary government planning instead of individual freedom, promises instead of prosperity. Socialism is a coercive society. Trade is not done voluntarily, but under force. Reason is abandoned for the gun. Socialism is based upon fundamental fallacies and must, therefore, create social disintegration.

The private ownership of gold is a roadblock to the schemes of would-be planners. The gold standard is an integral part of capitalism. As such, the principles of the gold standard must be understood, or any freedom to own gold would result in economic chaos, for which the gold standard would be blamed. And all privately owned gold would again be confiscated and the gold issue defeated.

The gold standard is simple to understand. It is a hard-money standard, which cannot be printed or otherwise manipulated by politicians. It frees that individual holder from the form of swindling and expropriations by the politicians. It keeps politicians honest. It is an essential safeguard for the preservation of the value of the currency and of human liberty.

Gold is the noblest of all metals. It is precious. Since it is almost indestructible, it has become a symbol of life. Gold in ancient times was equated with human life because it was used as a standard to measure the value of other things. And since it could be trusted to maintain its own worth, it was accepted in place of life itself. In fact, a gold ring was part of the price of buying a wife.

In modern times gold came to the rescue of American fliers that were forced down in the North African desert. In 1943, rewards of $1,000 gold were offered and paid for the assistance and safe return of American fliers.

More recently, the *New York Times* on July 16, 1967, printed the news that in 1967 American planes dropped millions of gold-colored leaflets over North Vietnam; they were captioned: "Reward—Fifty Taels of Gold—Reward." It explained that anyone helping a downed American flier escape could obtain this reward, about $1,760 in gold bullion.

Gold money is the money of last resort. It is universally

accepted. It is no accident that so many gold coins have survived from ancient times, or that gold coins of modern history can be found so frequently in brilliant uncirculated condition. It is the nature of the metal itself, as well as man's nature to desire to possess something of enduring value, that provides the answer. Gold is the key to confidence. What else has the reputation of honesty and integrity, and can be counted on to look and feel the same a hundred or a thousand years ahead?

The essential principles of sound money are impregnable. The gold standard lost popularity because for a very long time no serious attempts were made to demonstrate its merits and to explode the tenets of its adversaries. But the facts speak for themselves. Keynes warned that to destroy a country one had only to "debauch the currency." He was right. Since 1934, the American sense of life has been fighting gallantly for freedom from monetary despotism. If you wonder why the quality of workmanship has deteriorated, why job security has become an issue, why high unemployment continues to exist, why people are confused and frustrated with their jobs, their government, and themselves, take a good look at the value of the nation's currency. The nation is being ravaged economically and morally by inflation. The solution lies in the principles of sound money and in the Constitution—the law of the land.

The gold standard's time has come. The gold standard is the American way. It represents honesty and integrity. It deserves to be a major issue. Throughout our history the battle between hard money and paper money has raged. Hard money won in 1787, in 1832, and in 1900; it can win again. The gold standard is the most important issue of our time. Inflation will destroy the country. Only the gold standard can stop inflation. Eventually the future of the American dollar and of America's whole economic (and political) structure will be decided by those who control the world's gold.

Thomas Jefferson observed that mankind are disposed to suffer while evils are sufferable. Today, inflation is no longer sufferable. Fight for the gold standard, not as a "practical" issue, not as an economic issue, but, with the most righteous pride, as a moral issue. That is what the gold standard deserves, and nothing less will reclaim it. People must fight for something they want to achieve, not simply reject an evil, no matter how bad it is. Fight for the gold standard to reaffirm the virtues of which Americans are so proud: Reason, Justice, Productiveness, Freedom, and Achievement. What alone can prevent the United States from being enslaved by the barbarians of socialism and communism is open and unrestricted support of laissez-faire capitalism and the gold standard.

The time has come, said Governor Morris, one of the Founding Fathers, ". . . to raise a standard to which the wise and honest can repair . . ." He was speaking of the Constitution, of course. Today another standard needs to be raised, because Americans still suffer evils. This standard will end, once and for all, the despotic control over our lives and our property.

It is no accident that the nineteenth century is known as the century of peace and the gold standard. Likewise, it is no accident that the twentieth century, especially since the abandonment of the gold standard in 1933, is logically termed the century of inflation and war. The gold-standard issue must be raised. It deserves to be, can be, and must be a major political issue. Many Congressmen have already introduced gold legislation. They need support. This should be the most important issue of our time.

Everyone who works, saves, invests, or is retired, has a vested interest in the gold issue. Those being hurt by inflation have a powerful weapon at their disposal if they would only realize it and act accordingly. Once the people are aroused, politicians must pay attention. It is up to the people to demand the type of government and society they want. It is government's responsibility to protect the domestic tranquility. With economic stability would come political stability, with the possibilities of war drastically reduced.

The United States is at a philosophical crossroad. It is time for every American to take a stand. Either we return to first principles, to the Constitution, to the gold standard, or we continue down the path of least resistance and enter a coercive society.

As an illustration of the difference between the two types of societies compare the following quotes:

> The power of coining money and of regulating its value was delegated to Congress by the Constitution for the very purpose, as assigned by the framers of that instrument, of creating and preserving the *uniformity* and *purity* of such a standard of value.—UNANIMOUS opinion of the U.S. Supreme Court in 1850. [Italics mine]

> Gold is not necessary. I have no interest in gold. We'll build a solid state, without an ounce of gold behind it. Anyone who sells above the set prices, let him be marched off to a concentration camp! That's the bastion of money.—Adolf Hitler[2]

How shocking it is to see how far down the path of dictatorship we have come. Today our government, including the Treasury Department, assures us that gold is not necessary. The government has no interest in it and eventually we will build a strong economy without it. How far will government go to preserve its anti-gold stand? How far can we afford to let it go before it will be too late to turn back? I submit that the time to take the proper action is growing short. True, to restore the once uniform, pure and valuable dollar will be a very painful process, but the alternatives are worldwide inflation, socialism, and political repression.

The road to economic health begins by recognizing gold. Then the gold standard must be made a popular issue. Inflation is certainly an issue (though not too popular), since its ruinous effects are constantly in the news (and our pocketbooks). Currency reform would restore respect for private property, constitutional rights, and honesty to the scale of human values. The gold standard is honest, fair, just, and effective. If it were pre-

---

[2]Hoppe, *How to Invest in Gold Stocks*, p. 99, quoted from H. R. Trevor-Roper, *Hitler's Secret Conversations* (New York: Farrar-Straus, 1953), pp. 104-5.

sented to the American people, there is every reason to believe that they would choose to support it.

Inflation is crushing the United States. To get out from under we must reform the entire monetary system. Today, as in the past, a sound money system is the condition of man's freedom and the key to his future.

SELECTED BIBLIOGRAPHY

The Declaration of Independence

The Constitution of the United States of America

Allen, Gina, *Gold!*, New York: Thomas Y. Crowell Co., 1964.

Hazlitt, Henry, *Economics in One Lesson*, New York: Harper & Row, Publishers, 1946.

_____, *Man Vs. The Welfare State*, New York: Arlington House, 1969.

_____, *What You Should Know About Inflation*, 2nd edition, Princeton, New Jersey: D. Van Nostrand Company, 1965.

Rand, Ayn, *Atlas Shrugged*, New York: The New American Library, 1957.

_____, *Capitalism: The Unknown Ideal*, New York: The New American Library, 1966.

_____, *The Virtue of Selfishness*, New York: The New American Library, 1964.

Rueff, Jacques, *The Age of Inflation*, translated by A. H. Meeus & F. G. Clarke, Chicago: Henry Regnery Co., 1964.

Rothbard, Murray N., *Depressions: Their Cause and Cure*, Lansing, Michigan: Constitutional Alliance, Inc.,

Sennholz, Hans F., *Inflation or Gold Standard?*, Lansing, Michigan: Constitutional Alliance, Inc.

Von Mises, Ludwig, *Human Action: A Treatise on Economics*, 3rd edition, Chicago: Henry Regnery Company, 1963.

_____, *Planned Chaos*, Irvington-on-Hudson, New York: The Foundation for Economic Education, 1947.

_____, *Planning for Freedom*, 2nd edition, South Holland, Illinois: Libertarian Press, 1962.

_____, *The Theory of Money & Credit*, new edition, Translated by H. E. Batson, Irvington-on-Hudson, New York: The Foundation for Economic Education, Inc., 1971.

I

0